MUSSOORIE MEDLEY

Tales of Yesteryear

MUSSOORIE MEDLEY
Tales of Yesteryear

GANESH SAILI

NIYOGI
BOOKS

Published by

**NIYOGI
BOOKS**

D-78, Okhla Industrial Area, Phase-I
New Delhi-110 020, INDIA
Tel: 91-11-26816301, 26813350, 51, 52
Fax: 91-11-26810483, 26813830
Email: niyogibooks@gmail.com
Website: www.niyogibooks.com

Text & Photographs © Ganesh Saili

Design: arrtcreations; Nabanita Das/Niyogi Books
Editor: Supriya Mukherjee/Niyogi Books

ISBN: 978-81-89738-59-4

Publication: 2010

Printed at: Niyogi Offset Pvt. Ltd., New Delhi, India

This book is dedicated to all those who once lived in Sailgarh and to those who still live there: my wife Abha, thank you for giving me all that space; our eldest daughter Tulika for bringing us Nilanjana Singh Roy; our younger daughter Tania for always helping me in my fumbles with new-age technology; and my sisters Lalita, Amita, Namita, Punni and Meera (our youngest sister, who has since passed on) who grew up under this roof. And it'd be most unfair of me to forget my stress busters—Kaali and Bhoori (my pets)—Welcome to the club!

Contents

Preface

$\mathcal{M}$y *Mussoorie Medley: Tales of Yesteryear* neither is, nor pretends to be a comprehensive history of Landour and Mussoorie. It attempts to bring to you dear reader some of the fun and games, *gupp* and gossip of our small station's history and share with you some of its troubles. Of all the hill stations established in the 19th century by the British, ours has a special character.

If you remember that Simla was the headquarters of the British Raj; Nainital, the summer capital of the United Provinces, while Mussoorie, always racier, ended up as a sort of pleasure dome for maharajas and military on rest, recuperation and recreation. Ever wonder why the twins, Mussoorie and Landour, are so very different from each other? The answer is simpler than it seems—Mussoorie succumbed to the immediate economic needs of the hour, while Landour clung on to pretensions of leisure and contemplation.

For Landour, still in love with its past, has old bungalows clinging on to their names. The roll-call includes Alyndale, Firs, Seaforth Lodge, Shamrock, Bellevue, and Oakville. Please forgive us, if at all, for some of our unpainted roofs. I admit they look like they have been hammered-out of rusted biscuit tins! Trouble is the early houses, covered with thatch, had leaky roofs that poured like sieves in the monsoon. Over a period of time, they were replaced by the ugly but practical galvanized tin-sheets. What happens, in our times, the owners often forget to put a lick of paint!

This minor aberration apart, the cantonment has almost escaped the developer's myopic gaze.

Climb up through the narrow bazaar and you emerge in a mountain-top world of deodar trees, church spires, flowering gardens and panoramic views. This is as close as you can get to unspoilt British India. Luckily, the army owns all the land here. There is a pretty good chance it will stay that way!

Staying that way too are the old churches: St Peter's (established in 1829); St Paul's (established in 1840) and Christ Church (established in 1836), having just been restored by public spirited individuals. Though the old Methodist Church in Kulri needs repairs, even a fresh coat of paint would do it good. You will find all that shines here are the brass plaques put up in fond remembrance of the servants of the empire who sailed across the seas to die.

Some of those who died here are going to be with us forever. The two cemeteries, our dominions of silence, on Camel's Back Road and the Upper Chakkar, are in pretty good shape. Unfortunately, you cannot say the same of the rest of Mussoorie. If one could somehow wish back the one-time British rulers of India, or the wealthy maharajas who flocked here to escape the heat of the plains, they would be hard put to recognise it.

Everything has changed. Even the old rickshaws of yore, drawn by sturdy, liveried hill men, have been replaced by the ordinary three-wheeled cycle-rickshaws. To say they clutter the Mall is a classic understatement. 'Old' Mussoorie has been swallowed up by the burgeoning middle class. Kulri Bazaar overflows with fast-food restaurants, souvenir shops; high-rise hotels block the breathtaking views of the white Himalayan crests on the one side and the Doon valley down below. You will gape at files of raffish hotels sprouting plastic palms, out of which at dusk, the hordes debouch out of their bedrooms straight on to the roads.

I should remind first time visitors, our station runs east to west—all length and not much width. What you see is what you get!

If only the tourist ventured out, broke free and set out to explore the extremities of the town—towards Bhadraj in the west or beyond

Jaberkhet along the road to Tehri, to the east. Unfortunately, this remains the exception rather than the rule. Our present-day arrival's must-do includes Kempty Falls, Lal Tibba and my guru, author Ruskin Bond! Poor man! How they test his patience! Especially when aroused bleary-eyed like a bear from his siesta as fond parents arrive at Ivy Cottage waiting for him to bless their children or get photographed in the middle of the afternoon. Never mind even if he is still in his pyjamas!

Few know, when he is not sleeping, Ruskin's a great film buff. He and many other old-timers like him wish the town's six movie halls had not downed their shutters!

Once upon a time, entertainment was promised even if you did not like the film. Take for instance the Electric Picture Palace that opened in 1912, the year electricity came to town. This was Mussoorie's oldest cinema hall. Years later, the basement reincarnated as the Jubilee Cinema. They forgot to fix the leak on Picture Palace's roof. Over many monsoons, the rusty water trickled down, staining half the silver screen brown... Yes! You could still see your film but half in black and white, and half in sepia tone!

Literally, the last of our cinemas, at the end of Camel's Back Road, on the ground floor of Summer House, was the Basant Cinema. Reincarnated as La Anjuman, the change of name did not help as the seepage of sewage from the surrounding hotels drowned out the station's last cinema hall.

᠅ ᠅ ᠅

There are some who believe that Mussoorie paid because of its easy accessibility. Indeed, it is the only hill station visible from the plains. Helter-skelter expansion left us grappling with traffic congestion and shortages of water and electricity. Often garishly painted hotels promise guests hot and cold running water but usually it is the poor guest who does the running around—with buckets of water, hot or cold.

What were the largest stakeholders in town, the 17 prestigious schools doing all the while? Couldn't they have bestirred themselves to make a difference? In the end, they did what the sahibs and brown sahibs have always done. Talk was cheap. So, they talked. There was ample time to stop it, had they wanted to. But they waited, talked a lot, not pushing hard enough. They made some of the usual noises while turning a blind eye to the frenetic rape of their environs, choosing the security of their own artificial bubbles. Other schools set up 'solely for the benefit of children of the poor, the orphaned and the impoverished' forgot the noble dreams of the founding fathers. They too went main-stream—joining the loot and scoot! And may the devil take the founders and our hill station!

♣ ♣ ♣

It is no great secret that Mussoorie has always been a 'Station for Scandal'. What it has kept to itself is the tale of its man-eaters (or shall we call them man-eatresses?) no Jim Corbett could have tracked down and shot. They are not in the alleys, the lanes or the abutting jungles like their feline cousins. Our denizens have more cunning, more wile than any self-respecting tiger or leopard prowling these hills. Across the years, grass widows were not the only ones looking for a fling and merry widows swelled their ranks.

Ironically, in a gossipy little town, where everyone knows everyone else's business, their depredations are covered in a conspiracy of silence. And then, there is just one more little secret! For some inexplicable reason, Landour has always had a tradition of gambling. Do not ask me why? All you will notice as you walk up the great ramp of Mullingar, is clusters of residents playing cards wherever there be shelter from the wind or a patch of sunshine in winter. Writing in Charles Dickens' magazine *Household Words*, January 30, 1858, Australian writer John Lang, describes a visit to Suakholi, then in the Tehri Rajah's territory, where he came upon the largest gaming den north of Meerut. 'In the hostelries or sarais, nautch-girls would dance the night away,' as the rich and famous (now outside the reign of British Raj and its brass hats!) gambled fortunes away. According to local lore, a fine summer palace on Camel's Back Road has been lost and won several times over.

Though in our story, set many a century later, the gambling carried on at what we shall call *Chachi*'s house. Rather amply endowed, fair, tawny-eyed *Chachi* (aunt), ran an open house for lovers of the infamous fifty-two playing cards, in a room above her provision store. Local shopkeepers would gather there hoping to make a killing. Only problem was that when she got a bad hand, *Chachi* was prone to dropping her *saree-pallu* (part of the traditional Indian saree, draped across the shoulder), exposing a perfect plunging décolletage. Drooling to distraction, our card-players would lose a perfectly winnable hand!

When she passed away in ripe old age, I am told two of her admirers wept inconsolably. Putting his arms around them, *Chachi*'s husband did his best to console them, whispering soothingly:

'Don't worry! In a few months I'll marry again!'

'That's all right for you!' they cried, adding: 'But what will we do today?'

I wasn't in the least surprised when as a tribute to her many-fold talents, the entire bazaar downed its shutters for the funeral!

Yes! Our Mussoorie and Landour are still a special place!

Ganesh Saili

Landour
April 2010

SECTION ONE

Mussoorie Medley

Tales of Yesteryear

Once upon a time in
Landour and Mussoorie

Who goes to the Hills goes to his mother!

*'They had crossed the Siwaliks and the half-tropical Doon, left Mussoorie
behind them, and headed north along the narrow hill-roads. Day after
day they struck deeper into the huddled mountains, and day after day Kim
watched the lama return to a man's strength. Among the terraces of the
Doon he leaned on the boy's shoulder, ready to profit by wayside halts.
Under the great ramp to Mussoorie he drew together as an old hunter faces
a well-remembered bank, and where he should have sunk exhausted swung
his long draperies about him, drew a deep double-lungful of diamond air,
and walked as only a Hillman can.'*

— Rudyard Kipling's KIM

PREVIOUS PAGE: *Old
bungalows clinging to the
hillsides by sheer willpower.
Immaculately whitewashed
houses with red roofs of
those early days were in
harmony with a pleasure
resort like Mussoorie. In
the hills, you could not
build just anywhere. Trees,
lawns and extensive grounds
provided the right
atmosphere of tranquility.*

PAGE 2-3: *In Landour
Cantonment, where building
is restricted, the 78 old
bungalows like Green Lodge,
still retain their old
world charm.*

PAGE 6: *A mantle of Lady's
Lace blooms all over the
hillsides of Landour in
the monsoon.*

Not till they were a mile high in the sky did the empire builders
feel really refreshed. At long last, the scorching sun and the
stifling dust faded into distant memory. The breeze soughing through
the pines brought on a wash of nostalgia—it was, after all to the British,
just like home!

Almost all the northern hill stations of Nainital, Ranikhet and Almora
came into being around the 1820s; Mussoorie had the unique advantage
of being on an outside spur of the lesser Himalayas, instead of being buried
and lost behind fold upon fold of mountains, as the other hill stations like

Simla, Dalhousie and Darjeeling. Situated at the extreme edge of the first northern ridge of the mountains, it looks down upon the plains as you would upon a large map. This means, you are not cut off from the world below or trapped in the mountains, and you have a great sense of freedom to be able to get away from it all, as it were, by mere choice.

Mussoorie is today just a six-hour drive north of Delhi—the most visited hill station of the relatively young state of Uttarakhand. Of course, this easy accessibility to a 12 kilometre ridge remains its chief bane, as millions of holiday-makers converge here in the summer months, turning the place into a crowded rabbit-warren.

Though, it was not always like this. If you so much as turn the clock back two centuries, you will find that all over the hills, from Dalhousie to Darjeeling, smaller settlements in the mountains grew into larger townships, and gave birth to our hill stations of today. In the beginning, Mussoorie too developed as distinct settlements perhaps not too unlike old English villages. Along the old bridle path from the valley of Doon, the traveller came up the hills from Rajpur to Jharipani, Barlowganj, Kulri and Landour. Each settlement had its own shopping areas, schools and post office. Time sanded them all, connecting roads improved and merged to give us the symbiotic twins: Mussoorie and Landour.

A 1970s view of Barlowganj, named after a Major-General Barlow who lived in Whytbank Castle (now pulled down for a hotel) on the old bridle path from Rajpur to Mussoorie.

All our summer resorts turned into hill stations in the 1820s, during the British Raj. No sooner had summer's first blasts, the dreaded hot winds, begun to wreak havoc in the Great Plains of India, the families of British colonials rushed straight for the hills in fright.

In the days of its infancy, Mussoorie filled up as women took to the hills like flocks of migrant geese. Here they settled in hotels and clubs or rented a house from April to June or sometimes, till the end of September. Obviously, there tended to be more women than men, but this was more-or-less balanced out by the fact that there was always a steady flow of young men, and this flow was not just of husbands either, who would come up for a couple of days or the two week leave to get away from the heat. In mid-June, the social life in the hills would reach a crescendo in the 'hill station week'. There would be a fancy dress ball, a bachelors' ball, an odd tennis tournament, a play or a farce and fancy fairs.

At the end of summer, Mussoorie would get its unique, local pre-monsoon showers, called the *chotta barsat,* which usually began in the third week of June; at this time, Mussoorie would no longer be as attractive. The hills would get enveloped in damp cold mist and rain, with hardly any respite from the dovetailing into the monsoon. Living up here without their husbands, the womenfolk either hung on until the end of October; or left in July and stayed down; or went down in July for a month and a half and came back up until the end of September.

If you were a die-hard, you weathered the monsoon but with the onset of winter, you stayed here only if you had to, and almost 90 per cent of the hotels and guest houses boarded up in the winter.

So up and down the foothills came 'the great transhumance'.

One has often wondered, where did Mussoorie get its name from?

Mussoorie's historians are convinced that the name derives from the *Mansur* shrub *Cororiana nepalensis* that grows on calcinated soil, where, no self-respecting plant would even dare put in an appearance. Indeed, you will still find old timers in the bazaar, who call the place *Mansuri.*

I do not hold favour with those who believe that the name Landour is drawn from Llanddowror, a village in Carmarthenshire in southwest Wales, no matter how exotic it may sound. Landour probably had humbler origins, having been born in the princely state of Landaura, near Roorkee. Landour was home to the early traders who made their way here, following in the footsteps of the soldiers heading to the Convalescent Depot at the top of the hill in the days of the East India Company.

In the beginning, the Landour hill was quite sparsely populated and to fill up the space, the military authorities invited civilians to move there and set up their homes. Subsequently, 78 bungalows were built on the Old Grant Terms of the Cantonment Act on land that was leased to the settlers. The rules were simple: 'Build your dream house, but it could be taken over by the authorities if the need arose. You would be compensated for the rubble value of your property and the land would revert to the Cantonment.'

A view of the uncluttered Library in its early days as seen from Dick Road.

Trim Lodge on the ramp of Landour, below Mullingar, was once Colonel Young's potato field. Today, it is the author's home.

These old bungalows were named after the native places of those who built them. Often you will find that though the old houses and estates have changed hands many times, in most cases, the old names have somehow, miraculously survived.

Take our house for instance. It is simply called 'Trim Lodge' (with Trim Cottage and Trim Ville just below us in quick succession on the same spur). Could there have been a 'Mr Trim'? For there is nothing really trim about this old rambling house (or for that matter even its present owner!) and try as hard as I could, there is no trace of a Mr Trim.

Just above us, precariously poised, are the remains of the old 'Mullingar'. If you were to judge it from its ruinous looks today, you would find it hard to believe that it were once a fine mansion and the first pucca building to come up in the station. The Irishman, Captain Young, who commanded the first Gurkha battalion in its founding years, built himself a shooting lodge here, naming it after the coastal town of Mullingar in Ireland, from where he came, and returned to 44 years later on retirement as a General. Legend has it that on dark, moonless nights, a ghostly rider astride a white horse arrives at the old Mullingar, ties his steed to the remnants of the old wrought iron railing, snaps to attention and Captain (or is it General?) Young waits for the parade of the Redcoats to begin!

Mullingar's many incarnations continued in the form of different hotels. These include 'the Caledonian' till 1884 run by a certain Mr MacFie, 'Imperial' by Messrs Porter and Zinch; 'Oriental' by Mr FH Treherne (who also managed the grand Charleville Hotel in Happy Valley at the other end of town). One of the most significant events in the history of Charleville Hotel took place in March 1905. The Princess of Wales, who later was to be Queen Mary, attended chapel in Standish Hall, a part of the Mullingar Estate, while staying at the Charleville Hotel, the only hotel in India to be so honoured.

To go a little further in time, Mullingar's many incarnations lumbered on. By 1885, it had turned into the Philander Smith Institute. And during the Second War, it was home to the Allied troops who flocked to the hills to recuperate. At the time of Independence, it housed refugees pouring in from Pakistan. Then, in the 1950s, Seth Chandersain of the Mansa Ram Bank took over the property. Soon after, the private bank collapsed, as they did with sickening regularity in those laissez faire days and the property devolved to a liquidator.

Could one of Young's friends from the Irish County of Trim have built our house? Hard to tell as the only trace in the record room of the Saharanpur *Kutchery* (The court) reveal that the last British owner was a certain Mr EH Cockburn, who, left the property to his sister by a will executed in her favour. She died intestate and Trim Estate, as it

Capt Young's home in the Mullingar has been through many incarnations: the Caledonian, the Imperial, the Oriental and is today back to where it began and is called Mullingar, once again.

Up this lonesome bridle path track, on horseback, palanquins and Mr Buckle's Bullock cart train, came Mussoorie's early pioneers.

INSET: *The rhododendrons are few and far between today. Most of the larger trees were felled for timber used to build the old homes.*

was then known, devolved to the Custodian General, who put it on the auctioneer's block.

Only Mr Cockburn's spruce trees on our little patio, three in all, have outlived it all. May they continue to flourish!

This very same story of the early builders was being repeated all over the Himalayan foothills. Those hardy pioneers built houses with whatever they could lay their hands on: the limekilns of Khatta-paani produced fine lime; gravel was mined locally; the rhododendron trees were handy for beams, while water came on pack-mules from nearby springs. From these locally procured materials, all the bungalows of Landour were built. Nostalgia must have played a big part in the naming of properties here. The Scots with alacrity named their Himalayan homes after their 'Glens' and 'Braes'. Scattered all over the hill station you will find names of bungalows prefixed with 'Glen' like Glenbrook and Glenhead. Another favourite name was 'Burn', and the word 'burn'

means a small stream. If you rush off looking for springs, streams or water-bodies near Wolfsburn, Scottsburn or Redburn, you will be in for a big disappointment—there obviously are none. They were named for purely sentimental reasons!

The English preferred to name their homes castles, and you will find plenty of them in and around the old bazaar—the Whytbank Castle, the Connaught Castle, the Grey Castle and even the Castle Hill Estate. The last one, the Castle Hills Estate, is now with the Survey of India and has reduced to two crumbling houses: Woodcroft and Greenmount. These were bought by the East India Company from Mr Bleden Taylor in 1853. It was here, after the Sikh Wars, that the last Maharaja of the Sikh Raj, the young prince Maharaja Dalip Singh was interned, before being sent off to England to become Queen Victoria's blue-eyed boy.

If you were to take a stroll down the Camel's Back Road, on the terrace, just below the lych-gate, you will find the grave of a Frederick E Wilson (1816-83) of Hursil, an English freebooter and entrepreneur, settled in Hursil, Garhwal. He was responsible for transforming the economy of this area and was therefore considered, by later day historians, as one of the pioneers of the 19th century. Shunned by his own countrymen, for going native by marrying an Indian, Wilson was loved by the mountain folk and soon acquired the imperial title of Raja Pahari Wilson, when he minted his own coins.

ABOVE: Mussoorie had just been on the map for 20 years when an English freebooter, Frederick E Wilson, better known as Raja Pahari Wilson, arrived to start a career in the Garhwal Himalayas–a story from rags to riches.

ABOVE LEFT: The Whytbank Castle, was home to Major-General Barlow, after whom Barlowganj is named. It was part of the Patrician Brother's Monastery, connected by a suspension bridge to St Fidelis School. Sold to a builder, it has since been demolished to make way for a hotel.

BELOW LEFT: Pahari Wilson coins were tokens he would give his workers, which they would exchange with silver rupees at the end of the season.

This rags to riches story began in the mess of the Convalescent Depot in Landour, where a garrulous bartender introduced him to the thriving trade in animal trophies. Haring off to the hills to the north, he initially made a living gathering pelts, trophies and birds. Later the expansion of the Imperial Railways created a huge demand for straight wooden sleepers and in an area where there were no roads, it was not possible to bring timber down to the plains. Wilson came up with the idea of floating timber down the swollen rivers from the Bhagirathi valley to Hardwar in the plains. This turned out to be a lucrative business and in the process, he became a very rich man, owning fine houses in Dehradun and Mussoorie.

Perhaps his single greatest achievement was the construction of the 350 ft suspension bridge that he threw across a gorge in the Jad Ganga at Bhaironghati, Uttarakhand, in 1858. We are told, initially the fainthearted refused to use the rickety contraption but Wilson would have none of that—he mounted his horse and galloped across the bridge! An early traveller tells us: 'Wilson's bridge is worthy of a place in my book of daubs… altogether, a wilder-looking chasm can scarcely be imagined, is a very rude one: a couple of slight spars, thrown across from rock to rock about two feet apart, and pieces of stick and plank laid upon them.' On the first Sunday of November 1864, three shepherds with their flock of 150 sheep and six dogs crowded the river bridge. A freak gust of wind came down the gorge, flipping the bridge, casting the sheep, dogs and men into the river down below. What happened to his 'bridge' you might wonder?

ABOVE: Pahari Wilson's calligraphed Will.

BELOW: Pahari Wilson's wife Sungrami aka Gulabi Wilson.

RIGHT: This nine foot crosscut saw lies in Raimata's House in Mukba village, Garhwal. Ironically saws like these wiped out dense forests through excessive logging in the hills. (Picture Courtesy: Robert Hutchison)

After this accident, the bridge fell into disuse and with no one to repair it, it simply fell apart.

If you walk down the bazaar past Castle Hill, below the Clock Tower, you will find the Parade Point House—this too once belonged to Wilson. Now why would a wealthy man build a house at the fork of a bustling bazaar? In his old age, Wilson married Gulabi, the pretty daughter of the drummer of Mukba village, in the Bhagirathi valley of Garhwal. Proof of this came from the antiquarian, Hugh Rayner, who generously sent me a photograph he had found in England. The legend below it read: 'Mrs Wilson—a Hill Woman.' It is clear from this picture that she was the real Mrs Wilson. However, the popular pictures of the couple, that adorns the Forest Rest Houses in the Bhagirathi valley, is

ABOVE: A 16-year-old Raimata, Gulabi's niece from Mukba, married Pahari Wilson of Hursil. (Picture Courtesy: Hugh Ashley Rayner)

ABOVE LEFT: Pahari Wilson's apples for sale just below Mukba village–home of his two wives.

BELOW: Pahari Wilson's home in Hursil, in the Bhagirathi valley of Garhwal.

of a stern, balding Wilson and his wife's young niece Raimata, whom he took as a second wife. When I referred to the picture that Hugh Rayner sent to me, I noticed, that Raimata is wearing the same jewellery as the real Mrs Wilson, a middle-aged Gulabi. It was now easy to unravel the mystery behind Wilson's desire for owning a house at the junction of Landour and Mussoorie—he wanted to ensure that the two ladies of his life, Gulabi and Raimata, could mingle with their own folks from the hills.

On the ridge below our home Trim Lodge, is another house, curiously called White Park Forest. It took me many years before I learnt that it was a chummery—where three men, Mr Park, Mr White and Mr Forest, lived together!

To begin with, Landour and Mussoorie, were not together. They were entirely separate. The Convalescent Depot was on top of the Landour hill while Mussoorie showed a tendency to expand to the west, across the spine of Kulri Hill along the Mall Road to the fork of the Library and then onwards past the Abbey in the direction of Sir George

A welcome to His Holiness the Dalai Lama at the Tibetan settlement in Happy Valley.

Everest's home in Hathipaon (Elephant's Foot) towards Cloud End, near Benog Hill. This took in the entire expanse of Mussoorie. At the eastern end of the Mussoorie ridge, near Jabbarkhet, is an abandoned property popularly called the 'Haunted House'. How did it get its name? No one seems to know for sure. In 1888, Wynberg-Allen School was housed there. It caught fire and the property lies abandoned to this day. Up until the 1960s, it was a favourite lovers-haunt. At the western edge of the hill station is Cloud End. Between the two extremities were built the bazaars of Landour, Kulri, Library and Happy Valley.

The arrival of the first English visitors pre-dates the birth of the hill station of Mussorie to 1807, when the Governor General of India authorised the Survey of India to explore and map the upper reaches of the Ganga. Two people named Robert Colebrook and Webb were assigned this task. However, for their security, they sought the services of a man who knew the area well. Such a man they found in the dashing Captain Hyder Jung Hearsey. Born in 1782, in India, he was a loyal and devoted servant to King George and his successors, and offered notable service to them. Given his warrior-like demeanour, he could only have been cut out for the army. At the age of 16, he joined hands with Saadut Ali Khan, the ruler of Oudh. In mid-March 1808, Hearsey took the party of surveyors and set out over the foothills, through what was then Gurkha territory. At Haridwar, they secured the reluctant permission of the Gurkha Governor of Srinagar. The Gurkhas, as occupiers of the territory, tended to suspect all strangers as spies. Hearsey's group skirted the traditional pilgrim route along the holy river and crossed the valley of Doon, scampering up goat trails to what 20 years later would become the hill station of Mussoorie. From the bend in the upper reaches of Landour, near Lal Tibba, they had their first view of the Garhwal Himalayas—those angry fangs rising into the blue, spreading themselves like a mighty barrier of over a hundred miles across the north. They saw it as, 'A sight the most sublime and awful that can be pictured to the imagination.'

FOLLOWING PAGES (30-31): From the ridge at Lal Tibba opens a stunning vista of the mountains stopped only by the permanent snowline of the Himalayas.

It is significant to highlight the role of Young and Shore towards the making of Mussoorie. In 1823, there was just one house in Mussoorie, a hut or a shooting-box on Camel's Back Hill, put up by Mr Shore, the Assistant Collector of the Doon.

In 1827, the East India Company established a Convalescent Depot for British soldiers at Landour, with Captain Young as its first Commandant. In 1828, he built the forgotten St Peter's Roman Catholic Church on the ridge above the Cheh Tanki Flat, which takes its name from the boiler-like six tanks for water supply in the Cantonment. Landour's first private pucca building was Mullingar built for the personal use of Captain Young. Interestingly, just after the Irish famine, Captain Young began his experiments with introducing potatoes to the Garhwal Himalayas, on the flat around his home.

As officers, Shore and Young were as distinct as chalk and cheese. While Young had enlisted as a 15-year-old ensign, who had worked his way through the ranks, Shore, the son of a Governor General, remained strictly upper drawer. We find Shore belonging to a class of officers who played the game of the Empire strictly by the Marquis of Queensbury rules. This genre of administrators was destined, some feared, to become extinct.

Young had a great time as he divided the vast open lands of the Doon valley into plots, calling them 'Grants'. This arrangement, he palmed off to his superiors as the best way to get a firm grip on the new territory. But in doing so, he was most generous, especially to himself. When the matter was brought to the attention of Metcalfe, the Resident in Delhi, he was most upset. He had been cut out of the deal, left in the cold as it were by his subordinates, and got nothing. So, like a good servant of the not-so-honourable John Company, he fell back on the old ploy of being fair to all—he gave the Grantees an option—either keep the Grants or work for the East India Company! You could not have your cake and eat it too they were told! Understandably, Young was most reluctant to surrender his Grant. If next time you fly into Jolly Grant Airport, also known as Dehradun Airport, remember that there was no Jolly Grant. It was just a Mister or Major Jolly who had been given the grant of acres of land 200 years ago.

View of Landour from Mullingar, what was once a potato field.

At times, one gets the feeling that Young gets too much credit for his role in establishing the station. But through the haze of history, one thing is certain—Shore was cut from a different matrix. Writing about the essential qualification for a good district officer, he wrote: 'Not so much great talent as a determination to submit to perpetual annoyance in various petty ways.'

He was full of physical energy and unceasingly devoted that energy to the performance of his duty and the benefit of others. Frequently, his loyalty towards his employees went beyond the narrow confines of performing his duty.

He gave money to build the Doon jail out of his own pocket, and, after the settlement of the European residents at Mussoorie and the establishment of the Convalescent Depot at Landour in December 1827, that had increased the influx of visitors from the plains, his generosity extended to having shops set up along the roads for the comfort of travellers. This was done by means of advances, and, paying a headman whose duty was to supply labour, for which the demand had suddenly risen to a degree probably unprecedented in these provinces.

In those days of the freebooters, he remained a much-misunderstood man. For instance, he ruled in favour of the village folk of Kyarkuli when the newcomers simply usurped their hereditary flat lands in the new station. 'Make your own flats', he told the newcomers, 'do not take what is not rightfully yours!' But Shore's tenure was to be cut short. A curt official communication was to change the course of the hill station's history. It simply said:

> 'Mr Shore having embarked for England, I am directed to acquaint you that the Governor General-in-Council had been pleased to appoint Major F Young of the 68th native Infantry, Commanding the Sirmur Battalion, to be Superintendent for the affairs of Dehra Doon and its dependencies, and the Political Department as Superintendent of Jaunsar and Bawar.'

In Young's time, the District Magistrate and Collector of Revenue of District Dehradun was designated as Superintendent of the Doon because he was responsible for police duties too in Jaunsar-Bawar, a village about 15 km from Mussoorie. Young was appointed on a salary of Rs 500 per month while Shore, who was only Assistant Magistrate and Collector of Dehradun, was paid Rs 1,500 per month. Young's charge of the District lasted 15 years, from 15th August, 1826, till 30th December, 1841, perhaps the longest period that any officer had held this appointment. Some suspect that this disparity in the pay of the two, smacks of favouritism. Could it be that Shore's father had some influence with the Directors of the Company?

Fathers and father-in-laws, or just plain nepotism could have been the flavour of the season, even, in the brewing of alcohol. A brewery situated in the MacKinnon Park Area, had been started by Henry Bohle,

Beer bottling boomed in town in the 1830s. Messrs Murch and Dyer set up the Crown Brewery. Up until the 1970's, the ruins were still there.

who had come up from Meerut, in 1830. However, that shut down in 1832 when the estate was purchased by a Mr Parsons who sold it in 1835 to John MacKinnon, Bohle's son-in-law. John MacKinnon, a retired army schoolmaster from Scotland, is credited with setting up Mussoorie's first school here, called the Mussoorie Seminary.

Maugher Fitzhugh Monk, a young teacher at the school in a letter home on 8th June 1840, wrote: 'MacKinnon, who has established the school, is making money fast, and is, as far as I am able to judge, a tolerably liberal Scot… He, like most of us, has his faults—certainly not amiable ones. He is self-willed, obstinate and passionate.' That is as close to the truth as anyone who knew MacKinnon came.

On the western edge of town came Colonel Wyshe, Commandant of Artillery at Fort William in Calcutta, who had built the Park Estate, near Cloud End in 1827. About this time Captain Kirke, and one or two others whose names are among the first in the old Municipal 'householders' register, had commenced building. It is recorded that a merchant named Lawrence came up in 1828 with a stock of miscellaneous goods for sale and built a hut for himself and his goods, on the Camel's Back Road. Evidently, there must have been something of a European population by that time to purchase from him.

Sir George Everest

One of Mussoorie's most celebrated and distinguished citizen was Colonel Sir George Everest, FRS, CB, Kt, the son of Tristram Everest, born at Gwerndale, Brecknockshire, on July 4, 1790.

In 1806, he came to India as a young cadet in the Bengal Artillery. As an assistant to Colonel Lambton, the founder of the Great Trigonometrical Survey of India in 1818, he was to find both his vocation and his avocation in India.

Though he was largely responsible for the Survey of India and had the world's highest peak, Mount Everest, named after him, perhaps his truest memorial remains to be the meridional arc of India from Cape Comorin to the Himalayas. The measuring of an arc of the meridian, which gives us the size of the earth and is the basis of all later day surveys, was a stupendous achievement.

'It was not Everest but his officers', wrote an admirer in 1905, gushing, 'who placed his name just a little nearer the stars than that of any other lover of the eternal glory of the mountains. There let it stay, in witness to the faithful work, not of one man but scores of men.'

Of that great peak, much had already been written. It was originally known as 'Peak XV', and the Tibetans still called it 'Chomolungma'. Legend maintains that a breathless official of the Survey of India,

Radhanath Sikdar, burst into his superiors' office to exclaim: 'Sir, I have just discovered the highest peak in the world!' The height was calculated to be 29,002 ft. It was at 11:30 am on 29th May 1953, when, two men for the first time stood on the highest point on earth. These two men were Sir Edmund Hillary and Tenzing Norgay, who had reached where no man had truly been before. This achievement was announced to the world during the coronation ceremony of Queen Elizabeth and it marked for the British an auspicious start to the second Elizabethan era.

Colonel Sir George Everest was appointed as the Surveyor-General and Superintendent of the Great Trigonometrical Survey by the East India Company. Everest chose Dehradun as the permanent head-quarters of the Great Trigonometrical Survey and it has been so since.

Yet, he too had succumbed to the lure of the mountains.

In 1832, Everest applied for permission to move a part of his office to the cooler climes of the hills to the north in order, 'To establish themselves at Mussoorie and fix until such time as the two northern sections of the Great Arc are brought to a satisfactory termination.'

He decided to move to Hathipaon, 7,080 ft above sea level, building his office and residence at the Park Estate.

In May 1832, Everest bought the Park Estate in Hathipaon from Colonel Wyshe, who, had built a house there in 1827. Records tell us that Captain Everest bought it from him 'at a very heavy price'. He was to spend the next 10 years of his life in India, with Mussoorie as his summer headquarters.

Everest offered to use his influence with the Superintendent of the Doon, Colonel Young, to obtain ground for building on the range west of the Park Estate and adjoining it, for any of his subordinates who would apply to him for permission to buy land from the local village folk. Mr Morrison, Everest's Office registrar, was accommodated in the old brewery of Henry Bohle, northeast of the Park, which had been taken on rent.

There has been some squabbling over whether Everest had a *biwi-khana* or a harem, in Hathipaon. Definitely a big deafening, 'No!' For those who knew of Everest's stern, disciplined and uncompromising nature, dismiss these tales as a sort of wool-gathering in the Himalaya. He was too much of the patriarch to his juniors to indulge in anything else but the great survey.

The man had only one obsession in his life and that was to train young men in survey work. He gave permission to his subordinates to build temporary structures for themselves on his estate but on the express condition that they would vacate the place and remove all structures on a two months notice. He took exception to the fact that everyone seemed to call the junior workers in the survey as coolies. Everest's firm insistence on their being called *Khalassies* (attendants) seemed to have prevailed to this day. Everest also defended his surveyor's practice of distilling moonshine from wild plants in the forests for their own consumption.

As the civil and military officer at Dehradun, Young was Everest's senior by four years, and the saga of their dispute could well form the basis of a case study on the British stiff upper lip.

In her delightful piece on Dehradun, published by the British Associations of Cemeteries in South East Asia, Aylmer Jean Galsworthy discovers an exchange of correspondence between Young and Everest. Apparently, Everest received some paper regards his pension, which addressed him as *Kumpasswala* alluding to the surveyor's constant use of a compass. He dashed off an irate note: 'I am not a *Kumpasswala* but Surveyor General and superintendent of the Great Trigonometrical Survey of India. These are the appellations by which my masters address me, and no person has a right to withhold them from me.'

'As I never apply nicknames to any other person, and studiously avoid giving offence to others, I have a right to look for equal courtesy in return, and I hope you will prevent such offensive epithets appearing in any public paper intended to meet the eye, or wherein I may be spoken of.'

Frederick Young, the founder of Landour, joined the services of the East India Company as a 15-year-old cadet and was in service, without break for 44 years. When he left, he was a General.

Young reacted tactfully to this, pointing out that he did not notice anything disrespectful in the papers sent to him. His argument was that after all, *Kumpasswala* was the designation commonly applied to the Survey Department in this part of the country, and said, 'If for a moment I could have supposed it likely to give offence I should have ordered it to be corrected. I feel convinced that no disrespect could have been intended on the part of the petitioners, because they could not possibly gain anything by this insolence... I have given directions that no public document shall pass my office in which you are designated by any other title than Surveyor General Sahib Bahadur.'

But Everest would not let matters rest. He said: 'I never entertained the belief that you intended me any offence... I objected to a low, familiar, appellative which, though it may be in common use in the bazaar, I cannot allow to be applied to me as my official designation. The Commissioner... always designates me in his *parwanas*... by the title of Surveyor General Kishwar Hind, which is a literal translation of that assigned to me by my masters. I shall be obliged by your adopting that designation.'

With the controversy over the 'Affair of the Titles' barely behind Everest, trouble came from an unexpected quarter—this time it was objections from rich households over the occupation of vantage points by surveyors which, sometimes, provided a grandstand view of the *zenanahs* or the ladies section of the house. Of course, these wishes had to be respected, but a cantankerous Everest could not resist taking a pot shot at what he thought were ridiculous requests. His pen spat venom: 'The Surveyor should withdraw to a less convenient situation, where he might build a tower to any height he liked. The cost of the move would be paid for. The Zamindar must have money in superfluity to be willing to incur so vast a charge for an object as insignificant as that of removing ten or twenty paces. An edifice which, since it must surpass all circumjacent dwellings would equally command a view of his *zennia* for people disposed to be impertinent and curios at the distance of quarter of a mile.'

'But the persons of the Great Trigonometrical Survey are too good to concern themselves with Zalim Singh's *zenana*, and he does not do them justice.'

In a mocking tone he carried on: 'Persuaded that our telescope which invert have magic powers, and are able to turn women upside down (an indecent posture no doubt and are very shocking to contemplate), it is natural enough that they should assign to us the propensity of sitting all day long spying through stone walls at those whom they deem so enchanting.'

'But the Great Trigonometrical Survey is a department of hard work, with barely time for sleep or meals, have rarely leisure for such trifling as Zalim Singh anticipates, even if their taste were so ill-regulated, and their lot so forlorn, as to become prey to speculative amusement.'

The property at Hathipaon gave Everest a few headaches—the road was too slippery for riding horses and water was a constant source of worry—it had to be carted up the precipitous path on mules from the nearby springs, and, a few years later, he found himself struggling with the approach road. Of course the omnipotent rulers of the British Raj would have none of this.

Despite all of these inconveniences, this place was still Everest's preferred location to build an observatory and a large workshop but the government turned down his request. He kept trying, hoping against hope that the powers-that-be would relent, but that did not happen. On February 1834, an order was issued forbidding all civil and military departments to move their offices from the hills to the plains.

In September 1843, Everest left India, appointing Captain Murray, his neighbour, as his attorney to sell the Park.

Back in England, in 1844, he got married in 1845, at the age of 55. His wife Emma Wing was half his age. They had six children. He spent the autumn of his life with close, illustrious friends like Michael Faraday and David Livingstone, and died in London in 1866, at the age of 76.

After Everest left, the property became derelict in no time.

In the 1970s, in the heydays of the limestone quarries, the surrounding area of the Park was denuded, the earth gouged, Leopard Lodge vanished, and the Park was all but forgotten. Remains of an old structure, probably a storehouse for Everest's lumbering equipment or a work-shed to forge the tools for his Herculean task of mapping India, are all that are left.

After years of neglect, the Tourism Department 'discovered' Everest House and acquired it from a prominent lawyer of the Doon, daubed the old ruins with paint and now it lies mouldering under the vagaries of the weather. Maybe, someday, someone will wake up to find those countless tools of the early surveyor's trade.

Sir George Everest (1790-1866), the Surveyor General of India (1830-1843), bought the 600 acre Park Estate in 1832 and built his Hathipaon residence which now lies in ruins. Perched on the edge of a ridge in Park Estate are the remains of a house built by Sir George Everest. (Picture Courtesy: Robert Hutchison)

In September 1984, a tribal dance festival was organised on the spacious ground of Park Estate in honour of Colonel Sir George Everest. Folk dancers from all over India participated in the daylong festivities. Nothing of any consequence has happened in the Park since.

Could there be any better place to house a Museum of the Survey of India?

A shepherd's humble abode on the ground of Everest's Park Estate.

Everest had some illustrious neighbours at the Park Estate and they were William Fraser, the Resident of Delhi, owning Leopard Lodge, to the north and Major Swetenham, the Commandant of the Invalids Establishment at Landour, who owned Cloud End estate to the west.

The story of how Major Swetenham came to own the Estate reads like a fairy tale. Out hunting with his companions in one of the nearby villages, he was enchanted by the song of a highland-lass floating across the vale. He followed her home to discover she was the daughter of one of the local villagers. Knocked off his feet, Swetenham persuaded her father to allow him to marry her. Her father agreed and the local village girl became Mrs Swetenham.

The couple settled on her father's estate and built a house, which was called Cloud End, naming it after a peak opposite Swetenham's home in England. The couple had six sons, all of whom became Colonels in the British Indian Army. One of them, Colonel RA Swetenham, was a signatory to the Charter of the Dehradun Club in 1901.

In the course of time, Cloud End Estate devolved to two of the granddaughters of the original Swetenham's. One of them, Louise Swetenham, was popularly known as Mussoorie's 'Nightingale' while the other married the nephew of the Victoria Cross holder Raynor. In 1965, Colonel EW Bell, husband of one of them, sold the estate before leaving for England. Today, Digvijay Aggarwal runs a holiday resort here for those who prefer the quiet solitude of the hills far away from the clutter of Mussoorie.

Interestingly, it was Major Swetenham who bought the land of the 'Mussoorie Library' from Mr Scott and Mr Pitt. In 1843, a Mussoorie Library Committee was formed with Mr Vansittart, the then Superintendent of the Doon, as its President. In the very first year, the sum of Rs 2,500 was collected by way of subscription. Major Swetenham sold the land for a sum of Rs 300 and it was transferred in the name of Mr Vansittart, 'to be held forever in trust for, and on behalf of the Mussoorie Library Committee.' Today, the Library stands on the flat below the Savoy Hotel, opposite Bandstand. On the ground floor are shops, a source of income for the Library while the Library proper is on the first floor.

Of course, in the good old days, a band belonging to one of the British regiments, posted in Mussoorie, used to play for an hour every Wednesday and Saturday evenings. On these evenings, the upper verandah of the Library was hired to the Savoy Hotel and used as a restaurant. Ah! Those were the days of love and leisure, when there was time for the finer things of life!

Today, if you look closely at Bandstand, where, the army ensemble once used to strum its magic at dusk and from where sundry politicians address their rallies, you will find a fading inscription:

Erected 1915: This Bandstand was presented to the Mussoorie Municipality by H.H. Jagjit Singh Bahadur, G.C.S.I. Maharaja of Kapurthala.

The Oldest Himalayan Church

John MacKinnon, one of Mussoorie's leading luminaries was 'self-willed', obstinate and passionate' according to one of his employees in 1840. He started Mussoorie's first school, the Mussoorie Seminary, and went on to start a brewery along the MacKinnon-Cart Road.

PREVIOUS PAGE: A close view of the Christ Church.

If you take a walk down the Mall, the local promenade in Mussoorie, take time off from the tourist traps, drop out, and stop at Christ Church. You will witness the unique architecture of these houses of worship. They stand today in tribute to the religious concerns of those early founders of the town. Enter a charmed world where magic woven of sunbeams, with not a shadow of annoyance, filters through the splendour of stained glass. By 1835 the European population in Mussoorie was large enough to warrant the building of a Church. Soon the residents settled for a site on a hump above Kulri. Objections came from John MacKinnon, already a leading man in the hill station owing to his energy and public spirit, who felt that the Kulri Hill near Zephyr Hall would be too far a walk for the pupils of his school—The Mussoorie Seminary. He proposed that the new Church of England should be out to the west of the station. A compromise was affected between all the parties and the present site just above the Mall was chosen.

'It will be the first church raised amidst the eternal snows of Upper India,' gushed the Lord Bishop of Calcutta and First Metropolitan of India, in 1836. *In The Life of the Right Reverend Daniel Wilson, DD, Late Lord Bishop of Calcutta and Metropolitan of India*, we are told that: 'There was neither chaplain nor church when the Bishop entered Mussoorie. but he was a man of firm belief who seldom left a place as he found it!'

After performing a divine service for sick soldiers in the cramped St Peter's Church in the Cantonment, he decided to take things in hand. And the entries in his diaries say it all:

Tuesday, April 26th, 1836, 6.30 am: 'Very chilly morning, thermometer 44 degrees; driven in from my walk by the wintry cold. Yesterday also was cold, with a cloudy sky and rain. My poor torrified frame, accustomed for four years to excessive heat, is shrivelled up with this English January weather. But what a blessing such hills are! I was sitting, about eleven o'clock, with two or three gentlemen who had called, amongst whom was Captain Blair, just returned along the hills from Simla, when the two leading persons at Meerut, Hamilton and Hutchinson, came to talk with me about the church of which I gave notice on Sunday. We soon warmed. Plans, sites, architects, means of supply, were arranged in about two hours. I promised one thousand rupees from the Christian Knowledge Society, and two hundred rupees myself. Before night Mr Bateman, my chaplain, had sketched an elevation for a church, fifty feet by twenty-five, to hold two hundred people; and I had finished my letter to Mr Whiting, the owner of the land.

We shall have a church here presently. The beautiful plan was entirely approved by the Committee here on Monday, as well as by a scientific officer at Saharunpore to whom it was submitted. The estimate is three thousand two hundred rupees; and the subscriptions already raised, amount to three thousand three hundred rupees.

God be thanked, I have just returned from measuring out the site for our new church, to be called Christ Church, which Mr Proby had given us out of his own garden, about one hundred feet by sixty. This will be the first church built in India after the pattern of an English parish church. It will stand on a mountain like Zion 'beautiful for situation.' The tower is eighteen feet square, and thirty-five feet high. The body of the church is fifty-five by twenty three.

On Saturday we laid the foundation stone of Christ Church Mussoorie, the whole Christian population poured out; I suppose four or five hundred

persons. The scene on the gently sloping side of the hill was exquisite and the entire ground around the circuit of the foundations was crowded. The Himalayan Mountains never witnessed such a sight. I made a short address. The senior civilian, Mr Hutchinson, next read the deed of gift. Colonel Young, Political Agent (the King in fact of the Dhoon) read a copy of the inscription. All was now ready, and I descended into the deep cavity in the mountain and laid the stone in the name of the Father, the Son, and the Holy Ghost. The Lord's Prayer and Benediction closed the service. As we were departing, the band of the Ghoorka regiment struck up the National Anthem, which echoing and re-echoing amongst the mountains, was the finest thing I ever heard. Afterwards I entertained the Committee at dinner. We sat down, twenty-one, in camp fashion—each one sending his own chair, knives, forks, plates and spoons. God be magnified! The whole celebration was unique. It will be the first church raised amidst the eternal snows of Upper India, and all planned, executed, and money raised in a single month. Nine months will finish it!'

We are told that Capt Rennie Tailyour, of the Bengal Engineers, Roorkee, built its tower and nave in 1836, the flat-roofed structure was consecrated by Reverend Wilson in April 1839. The chancel and transepts were added 17 years later in 1853 and the bell was presented by LD Hearsey, son of Hyder Jung Hearsey.

Walk down the aisles, the grace of the eight tapering windows will take your breath away. Consider the risks involved in transporting these treasures, then worth more than their weight in silver, their fragility and fury and violence, of both history and weather.

Bathed in the mysterious light filtering through bits of coloured glass, one suddenly comes face to face with the magic of rare charm and beauty—light that has finally come alive with the colours of the

FACING PAGE: Christ Church above the Library ridge soars into the sky. Consecrated in 1839, it was the first Church in the Himalayas.

BELOW: Christ Church chancel at the east end, where the choir and clergy once sat. (Picture Courtesy: Robert Hutchison)

The glory of old stained glass scatters the faith among the devout at Christ Church. ((Picture Courtesy: Robert Hutchison)

rainbow. You feel as if they had been made of jewels. At first glaziers made windows, and then relied on pieces of coloured glass to make a pattern. Painters came in to fill the need for art that the glazier lacked. From mere patterns treated with colour, they became pictures of saints and Biblical figures, with all sorts of settings and background. Special glass required more skill: the turquoise-blue or green was produced by the addition of copper; iron stained green; cobalt blue, iron and antimony together, browns and yellows; manganese stained amethyst and purple; the fine ruby-red you see is from gold chloride; the black is a combination of iron and manganese; the greenish-yellow titanium, red from selenium, purple and blue from nickel, yellowish-green from chromium. No hue is quite pure and the violet falls somewhere between lavender and grape-jelly purple while the yellow tilts toward chartreuse, and the green favour dusky teire verta. As for white, also known as milk-and-water glass, tin oxide was preferred.

On a superficial level, you might wonder what is all this fuss about? Is it not just your ordinary windowpane given a touch of colour by adding some metallic oxide or by burning some pigments into the surface itself? Not really. These pieces were put together one at a time like a jigsaw-puzzle with bands of lead to give them some sort of unity.

When done, they accumulate a force of subtle, drenching emotion. It is a symphony of colour, a moveable feast for the eyes, the drama of their colours, the rainbow's sequence of primaries and secondaries, advancing from violet, which is usually the ground colour, through blue, green, yellow, orange and red.

You could say the same of the pipe organ here. 'Make a joyful noise unto the Lord, all ye lands' proclaims Psalm 100.1 and to ensure that this invocation was not lost, a William Hill pipe organ was brought to the Church in the 1880s. For the past 50 years and more, it has been silent. On a recent inspection, Sebastian Meakin, a restoration expert from JW Walker & Sons, UK, declared the Church Organ to be 'of exceptionally high quality and historic interest.'

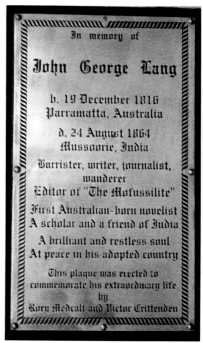

In memory of

John George Lang

b. 19 December 1816
Parramatta, Australia

d. 24 August 1864
Mussoorie, India

Barrister, writer, journalist,
wanderer
Editor of "The Mofussilite"

First Australian-born novelist
A scholar and a friend of India

A brilliant and restless soul
At peace in his adopted country

This plaque was erected to
commemorate his extraordinary life
by
Rory Medcalf and Victor Crittenden

*ABOVE: This rare portrait of
the Prince of Wales adorns
the Masonic Lodge as
memory of his Mussoorie
visit. (Picture Courtesy:
Robert Hutchison)*

*RIGHT: Plaque on a tree in
Christ Church.*

*EXTREME RIGHT: A memorial
plaque on the walls of Christ
Church is a belated tribute
to John Lang, the Australian
writer who made Mussoorie
his home. (Picture Courtesy:
Robert Hutchison)*

History lies littered all around and even in the churchyard. As you step out, stop under the spread of the huge deodar tree where the plaque on the railing reminds you:

> *THIS TREE WAS PLANTED BY H.R.H. THE PRINCESS OF WALES*
> *ON SUNDAY MARCH 4TH 1906*
> *AFTER ATTENDING MORNING SERVICE AT CHRIST CHURCH*

This was Her Royal Highness Mary of Teck, who visited Mussoorie as part of a grand tour of India with the Prince of Wales. In 1920, he became George V.

Back on the Mall, the lines of Walter de la Mare come back to me:

'Look thy last on all things lovely,

Let no night seal thy sense in deathly slumber

Till to delight

Thou hast paid they utmost blessing.'

Nutty, Naughty Mussoorie

*J*f we go by the British chroniclers of the minutiae of their lives, one discovers that, apart from seeking spiritual healing and strengthening faith, people came to Mussoorie with 'other' things on their mind. Mussoorie was thought of as a naughty place, where apparently, you did your own thing. Nothing illustrates this better than a report in *The Statesman* of 22nd October 1844:

> 'Last Sunday sermon was delivered by the Rev Mr Hackett, he chose for his text Ezekiel 18th 2nd verse, "The fathers have eaten sour grapes and set their children's teeth on edge." The right reverend discoursed upon the highly immoral tone of society up here, which it far surpassed any other hill station in the scale of morals; that the ladies and gentlemen after attending church went on to a drinking shop, a restaurant adjoining the Library and there indulged freely in pegs, not one but many; that at a Fancy Bazaar held this season, a lady stood up on a chair and offered her kisses to gentleman at Rs 5 each. What would they think of such a state of society at home?'

The Reverend's admonition seemed to have very little effect. As late as 1932, a charity saw a lady auction a single kiss for Rs 300! Ah! What a sad commentary on the inflationary trends of the times!

The bold, bad, good old days make today's Mussoorie look like a pale imitation. You will not get even a whiff of the fragrant *mogras*', a variety of jasmine flower, in the air today, where once guests would

PREVIOUS PAGE: The romance of hand-pulled rickshaws died out in the late 1980s.

FACING PAGE: An unknown peanut vendor from the early 1970's would set up his stall near the Landour Post Office in the season. A familiar sight to residents and visitors till he did not return one summer.

have lounged around on one-mound mattresses listening to the *mujra* or the song and dance of Shailja of Benares at hotels like the Savoy, the Hakmans or the Paladium.

Quietly, without a murmur, the station continued to grow—from just 141 houses in 1862, the station had 351 houses by 1881! So, sanitation was to become a major problem. Arriving in India in 1822, Fanny Parkes, the wife of a junior English civil servant, spent 22 years travelling in the countryside having fallen in love with the area. She wrote a book called *Wanderings of a Pilgrim in Search of the Picturesque*, in which she mentions the outbreak of cholera in Landour Bazaar around 1840, that made most of the hill bearers to take flight.

This news of the outbreak of cholera did not spread for the simple reason that the station had no telegraph. That had to wait till 1865.

No one of any consequence who came to the hill station after 1841, when the Himalaya Club threw open its doors in 1841, could afford to ignore this hub of social activities. Colonel Frederick Young, Colonel Proby Cautley and John Lang were some of its earliest members. (Picture Courtesy: Hugh Ashley Rayner)

But the stations other landmarks continued to grow. A Roller Skating Rink was built by Dr Miller, a prosperous dentist. It is rumoured that he was given the site in 1890, by one of his patients who was unable to pay for services rendered. Though, just four years down the road, the venture fell apart, to be snapped up by Charlie Wilson, one of the sons of Rajah Wilson of Hursil.

By 1900, the opening of the Hardwar-Dehradun railway line, made Mussoorie the most accessible hill station in northern India. It was faster, it was easier and cheaper for train-loads of women—some with their husbands and children, others 'grass widows' whose husbands had to stay at their jobs in the plains, some real widows and other eligible females fishing for husbands, to take to the hills in summer. Although, very soon, almost every hill station was well within the reach of a railway terminus.

To escape the summer heat, these flocks of visitors would get through the summer months in Mussoorie, spending time in all kinds of frivolous activities. After all, the town had two breweries, a polo ground, a six-hole golf course, the Happy Valley and the Himalaya Club to turn to.

Fancy Dress Balls with Egyptian dancers were very popular in the late 1920s.

Soon, the princely homes began to dot the landscape. A little way up the Savoy Hill, arose the imposing turrets of a French castle—the imperial residence of Maharaja Jagjit Singh of Kapurthala's Chateau. Around the pleasure dome was scattered spacious tennis courts, manicured gardens where the cream of Mussoorie's aristocracies flocked for fancy dress balls, dinners, suppers and tea parties almost seven days a week. Through its gates streamed British officers with their English companions and the crème de la crème of Indian society. Copious amounts of food and alcohol flowed at these events with the couples wandering around the vast grounds. Tales of these wild, wild bashes all over the station, carried all the way to Simla, the then summer capital of India, which did not amuse the brass hats. Naturally, Mussoorie had soon picked up a reputation of being a frivolous place full of gaiety and laughter.

And they tell us of the 'cool', swinging Mussoorie of the 1920s. Ballroom dancing was the rage. At the Stiffles and the Hakman's Grand Hotel, the special nights were so popular that tables overflowed on to the pavements. There were dance-teachers of German descent—Mr Roberts and his wife, a well-known dancing couple who resembled Fred Astaire and Ginger Rogers, movie-stars of yesteryear's. The couple helped you dance the night away.

What became of our dancing gurus? Mr Roberts went back to Europe after the end of the Second World War, where collecting his share of war-reparations, he died most suddenly, some say at the pension counter. His widow continued to receive the proceeds of this money, living like a recluse till ripe old age with a menagerie of pet dogs, and passed away unsung in 1987.

The Stiffles Restaurant, advertised as 'Come Where its Always Bright' was one of the best eateries in town. Many of the principal Catering Contracts during the Prince of Wales visit were undertaken by the 'Stiffles'. The building later became the Standard Skating Rink which perished in a fire in 1969.

Tales of the Old Savoy

𝓜y first brush with the fun and games that were a part of the station's history began in the early 1970s when I first met Anand Jauhar (better known as 'Nandu' to his friends). He had come home at last to his roots in Mussoorie, having spent an errant youth running a restaurant in London's Marble Arch. When I look back over the years, little did any of us, my friends or I, have an inkling that a chance meeting would change our lives irrevocably—forever! Nothing was ever to be the same again.

For come summer or winter, the old Savoy was a great watering hole. This was where Ruskin Bond, Mussoorie's resident author of over four decades, and I, met a whole gamut of characters: film stars, rogues, politicians, business tycoons, fly-by-night operators and some fast fading beauty queens!

Of course, if you were to dig around, you would still find their flourishes in the visitor's book. I last saw that well-thumbed tome on the Front Desk, to the left of Chatter Singh Negi, the octogenarian Manager of the Savoy (when he retired three years ago, it was rumoured that he had gone through two wives and 70 years in the hotel). Encapsulated between its green-and-gold covers was a veritable Who's Who of Mussoorie's early history: His Holiness the Dalai Lama and Panchem Lama, Haile Selassie—the Emperor of Ethiopia, Prince Norodum Sihanouk, and even members of the great Nehru-Gandhi family—from Motilal, Jawaharlal, Indira and down to Rajiv. All were guests at the hotel, who, could waken at dawn to see from their window, the long line of Himalayas spanning the horizon to the north while to the south stretched the Doon valley, where the winter line marked its presence on the horizon.

Right up to the 1960s, if you could not find a room at the Savoy, you had a choice between the imperial Charleville Hotel in Happy Valley, which became the National Academy of Administration, and the Hakman's Grand Hotel, in the middle of the Mall Road, which

The façade of the Savoy Hotel in the 1970s.

ABOVE: *The quiet walk along the Mall Road is a thing of the past, replaced by a raffish clutter of shops, stalls and even a ropeway up to the top of Gun Hill. In better days, the Municipal Act of 1916 ensured that all houses got a clear view of the Doon valley.*

RIGHT: *The Reception and Front Desk of the famed Savoy Hotel with its old railway-station architecture is an imprint of the Raj.*

lamentably has gone to seed. The Savoy, like a lost wooly mammoth, in a changing world, stumbled on.

Like other sprawling hotels, the Savoy once had a life of its own. There were rich patrons—usually the ex-rulers and landed gentry who, with their retinues, trooped through its gates. If the Wodeyars, rulers of Mysore, occupied a whole wing then the Gaekwads, the royals of Baroda, took over an entire block. In their wake, came the civil and military officers on furlough who partied till day break.

On my first visit, in 1978, I found a whiff of the era still lingering in the air. Breakfast, lunches and dinners were served with personal attention suiting individual tastes. There was nightly dancing in the ballroom. Cabaret artists of varied backgrounds chased the night away with their repertoire of songs, dances and striptease. There was frolic and fun: lawn tennis and squash, snooker and skittles, card tables and chess games and fancy dress balls. Close by was the old Mussoorie Library, established in 1834 that satiated the guests' fondness for reading.

The only constant in a sea of visitors, was the hotel staff. It had a firm pecking order, a sort of totem pole, starting from the manager,

down to the stewards, reception counter clerks, chefs, waiters, the night-chowkidar (watchman), the room boys, and the sweepers—each one claimed to be privy to some steamy secret surrounding the hotel and its numberless guests.

Often Nandu would get caught up in these games of fantasy. We discovered he had dreams for a grand future the beginning of which seemed to commence with the christening of the old Savoy bar. After all, he argued, what was a bar without a name? The thought had stolen upon him on a visit to the historic Raffles Hotel in Singapore, where in the Writer's Bar, brass plaques proclaimed Somerset Maugham had been there, as had, Joseph Conrad and Graham Greene. Finally, one day, Nandu threw the question at Ruskin Bond and me: why could the Savoy not have its own Writers' Bar too?

'Writers' Bar! Where on earth would you get writers from?' I asked.

'Well! Just for starters you two are there! Are you not a writer Ruskin Bond?' he exclaimed triumphantly, adding: 'Don't you fellows know some other writer types?'

'None! I am afraid. The Lost Weekend variety of dipsomaniacs are out of fashion!' exclaimed Ruskin. 'Why not just call it the Horizontal Bar instead?' But Nandu would have none of it. With a withering look, he careened on: 'They do not have to be the heavy boozer types only!'

Who could argue with that?

So, after much dithering and tippling, Ruskin and I simply capitulated. After all, a hotel with a hundred years of history behind it, there was no telling who could not have dropped by for a drink even if it were just plain *nimbu-paani* (Fresh limewater)!

Soon, the deed was done. Over the weekend, the wooden plaques were hammered together by the local coffin-maker and mounted on to the walls. They celebrate, the often tenuous link with writers like John Lang, the Australian-born novelist; Jim Corbett, the shikari (hunter) turned naturalist (whose parents married in St Paul's Church, Landour); John Masters who spent time with the Gurkhas

Anand Jauhar, also known as Nandu to his friends, was the last owner of the 21-acre Savoy hotel. The hotel is undergoing renovation.

A warm foyer welcomed the visitor to the Savoy Hotel in the good old days.

in the Doon; and even Pearl S Buck, the Nobel laureate, though she never wrote a word about our hill station! But she did stay at the hotel as the old register tells us.

It was not writers only who strayed into the old Savoy. To appreciate what the hotel was all about, you will have to travel back in time, and get a feel of the origins of the hill station.

As they say in fairy tales, once upon a time, Mussoorie too was 'the queen of resorts and the resort of kings', a sort of meeting place for the rich and the powerful. But the town was never really anything officious or stuffy. It was where you could find yourself sailing into a 'fishing-fleet' of young girls looking for eligible bachelors, or meet rakish bachelors whispering sweet nothings into the ears of grass widows under the eaves. And if you think, the husbands had run away or were absconding, you are wrong! Poor things were minding the affairs of the State in an Indian summer in the sultry plains! Mussoorie was, and to a limited extent, still is, a place where you can let your hair down without inviting social censure.

With the passage of time, the need arose for a place of quiet luxury. Cecil D Lincoln, a barrister from Lucknow, took over the lands of the old Mussoorie School, pulled down the school and built a hotel in its stead, naming it the Savoy after the Fayrest Manor in Europe. To his credit goes the English Gothic architecture, its fine proportions, its lancet-shaped narrow windows along the corridors and the veranda's. You can still find the original school emblem, a four-leafed clover, peeping out from among the eaves.

Two simple spires, without any parapet, surmount the corners of the main building—rearing their heads in pride. This constitutes the main facade. If you consider the fact that the first motorcar came to the hill station in 1920, you can only admire the sheer ingenuity and dogged perseverance of the early settlers. Men and materials came up the bridle path from Rajpur. Everything found its way up the winding serpentine trail by bullock cart. Massive Victorian and Edwardian furniture, billiard-tables, grand pianos, Burmese teak for the ballroom floors, rotund barrels of beer and cases of champagne and cognac—all the requirements of a fine hotel trundled up the hill on lumbering bullock carts.

Launched in 1902, the hotel was, as described by a local scribe—'like a phoenix rising from the ashes of a school'. Royalty was to grace the station four years later—Her Royal Highness, the Princess of Wales, later Queen Mary—attended a garden party in the Savoy grounds. No sooner had she left, a severe earthquake hit Mussoorie. Many buildings were flattened and the hotel suffered much damage and had to be closed for a year. But by 1907, the Savoy was up again, ready to witness some momentous events in store.

In between the two Great Wars, in the 'gay twenties', Mussoorie entered its days of wine and roses. In its heydays, the Savoy orchestra played every night, and the ballroom was full of couples dancing the night away. You could do the fox trot or waltz to the happy numbers, or just do your own thing.

On a visit in 1926, Lowell Thomas, in *The Land of the Black Pagoda* wrote: 'There is a hotel in Mussoorie where they ring a bell just before dawn so that the pious may say their prayers and the impious get back to their own beds.'

When I asked Nandu, he confirmed: 'They employed an old, short-sighted chowkidar to ring the separation bell at four every morning. It guaranteed absolute privacy to the guests as they scampered back to their own rooms!'

During the Second World War, the British and the American military officers, on leave, sought amusement in the hills and what

THE WRITERS' BAR AT THE SAVOY HOTEL

The Writers Bar at the Savoy Hotel salutes its association with these professional authors, who made a living exclusively from writing:

John Lang, author and barrister, spent the last five years of his life in Mussoorie from 1859-64. Apart from writing novels like 'Botany Bay & the Forger's Wife', he was a regular contributor to Charles Dickens' magazine 'Household Words'. Lang's grave is in the Camel's Back Cemetery.

Rudyard Kipling, England's first Nobel Prize winner for literature in 1907, describes 'the Great Ramp of Mussoorie' in his novel 'KIM'. Visiting Saharanpur, Dehradun and Mussoorie, he used his observations in depicting the journey with the Old Lama.

Jim Corbett's father was the Postmaster in Mussoorie, meeting his wife here; they were married in St Pauls Church in Landour. It was on the 2nd of May 1926, he shot the dreaded Man-eating Leopard of Rudraprayag, just over the next mountain ranges.

ABOVE LEFT: Ruskin Bond, Anand Juahar with friends—Allen and Angela Middleton at the Writers Bar.

ABOVE RIGHT: Author Ruskin Bond takes a closer look at the plaques that celebrated other writers' past and present.

BACKGROUND: The Doon valley lies below like star-showers—twinkling at night.

Philip Mason was Commissioner of Garhwal, writing seven books under the pseudonym Philips Woodruff including 'The Wild Sweet Witch'; 'Call the Next Witness', 'The Men Who Ruled India' and 'A Matter of Honour'.

Lowell Thomas the famous travel writer spent two years travelling 60,000 miles in India. He describes the Savoy separation bell in his famous book 'INDIA: Land of the Black Pagoda' (1930).

John Masters, the popular best-selling author of 'Bhawani Junction', 'Bugles and a Tiger', served with the Gurkha Regiment in Dehradun before and during World War II.

Charles Allen, author of 'Plain Tales from the Raj' & 'A Mountain in Tibet' was born in India where six generations of his family served during the British Raj. He stayed at the Savoy in Suite No 1 in the 1960s.

Pearl S Buck, Nobel Laureate 1931, author of 'The Good Earth' and other novels stayed in Suite No 8 of the Savoy in 1959 when she came to meet HH the Dalai Lama.

Peter Hopkirk stayed in the Savoy when researching for his book 'In Search of Kim'. Among his popular books are 'The Great Game', 'Foreign Devils on the Silk Road' and 'Trespassers on the Roof of the World'.

Ruskin Bond author of a hundred books has spent over thirty-five years in our hill station & forms the background for many of his stories and novellas. Many of his stories are set in the Writers' Bar.

ABOVE: The Writers' Bar would fill up at dusk in the last few days of its glory.

could be a better place than the Savoy. Legend has us believe that the sale of whisky used to be so high that Lincoln would have all the empty bottles from the previous day's sale, collected and brought down to the cellar. Gently he would coax every last drop of scotch from each bottle. Miraculously, he would have two full bottles ready for free-loaders and house guests the next day!

Though, it was not all about tippling alone. Sometimes guests would be staggered by the size of the luxury suites: Number 1, Number 8, Number 4 and Number 5. I was once told, that when the hotel was almost full one day, an elderly couple was shown the last available

The Savoy Hotel was a great place to have fun. It was where the famous met the infamous, the beauty queens met the lover boys and romance was in the air.

room—the bridal suite. 'What will we do with this?' the old man exclaimed. 'Sir! If you are shown the ballroom, you do not have to dance!' said the ever-resourceful Chatter Singh Negi.

Nandu's father, holidaying in the hills a year before Partition, bought the 21-acre Savoy complex in 1946. Till just four years ago, the Savoy was still a family-run hotel, when due to a bout of ill-health, Nandu gave up his shares to the new owners. At present, they are trying to update it with some modern-day creature comforts, without changing the contours of this fine heritage hotel. One wishes them luck in their endeavours!

On my last visit there, I had finished making pictures, I bid farewell to the charming old billiards room (where in 1900, a leopard was found hiding under the rosewood table) and try to catch some of the spirit of the heydays of the British Raj. I remind myself that the history of Mussoorie must have wandered through the Savoy's vast spaces. I walk down the rambling corridors, the empty sun-drenched lounge, lost in memory of happy times, and just then Nandu catches up with me. Together we

LEFT: Old billiard rooms like these provided in-house entertainment to guests at the Charleville and Savoy Hotel.

RIGHT: The teak floor dining room of the Savoy during the days of its glory. It had all the appurtenances of the British Raj: Victorian and Edwardian furniture, grand pianos and even billiard-tables.

At night the Savoy evokes nostalgic memories of its heydays.

walk through the deserted dining room. He jokes, 'This hotel is so big that by the time you get to the room from the reception, we could have charged you for a day!'

Going past the Writers Bar, a wave of nostalgia washes over me, I tear myself away, rushing down the steps—those familiar twenty steps, one last time. How well I know things will never be the same again There are new owners now and no one knows what the future holds.

Suddenly, I hear a shuffling behind me. Is it the ghosts of the past come to bid one last goodbye? Or is it the wind playing in the gables? Who knows? I move on from door to door, from transept to transept, from corridor to lounge, from ballroom to balcony, tracing a century here and a generation there, in pillar and arch, vault and buttress. And I will probably end where I began: at the rosewood entrance which throws its massive arch into a work-a-day world, and inside, hoards a treasure trove of memories. Brimming over with the sheer loveliness that comes from wood and stone!

And for over a 100 years, emperor and clown have walked up these very steps, through this very same arch into a magnificent doorway to history! The Savoy still appears, at the time of one last farewell, like a shimmering mirage in the memories of those who resonated to its poignant beauty years ago.

Shutterbugs of
Our Hill Station

O ur perch in the Himalayas has always been home to those who 'write with light'. Foremost amongst them is Samuel Bourne who in the Photographic *Journey in the Himalayas* (1863) left us three dozen pictures of these hills. This 29 year old bank clerk left us a vivid record of the station in the days of its infancy. Close behind him, almost snapping at his heels was Thomas Alfred Rust (TA Rust), with landscapes from the 1865. Later his son, Julian Rust left us images of the 'Gay 1920s'.

In their wake came the deluge: the Kinsey Brothers, Doon Studio, Mela Ram & Sons, Bhanu Studio, Hari Saran, Bora's Studio (whose

With wooden-railings in the foreground, the road slithering down to the plains. This sepia-toned imprint is from TA Rust's collection (circa 1870s).

PREVIOUS PAGE: *Anyone will be charmed by mist in the hills but in 1835, a Baron Carl Hugel tells us, that it rained non-stop for 85 days with a few hours break in between!*

1930s death-mask of the jeweller Janki Das, still adorns his silver-shop in Landour) and the least glamorous of them all, Glamour Studio, still survives opposite the second-hand shop near the Clock Tower.

No one will tell you how the 40-odd photography, shops began. Together they constitute the largest congregation of *photowallas* in any hill resort in the world. They are adept at turning your fantasies into reality: dressing eager honeymooners in outlandish hilly-girl (sic) dresses or turning them into Chambal dacoits, a la Gabbar Singh from the block-buster Bollywood film Sholay—complete with bandolier and gun!

Photography had made not the great leap forward but crossed the river by stepping on one stone at a time.

Post partition 1947 onwards:

Thukral Studio in London House near Picture Palace was the Mecca of photographers, both big and small. They made great pictures of school fancy fairs, debates, class groups and sport events. But they kept weekends for themselves, taking nature pictures around the Upper Chakkar in Landour.

LEFT: Picture Palace as it was in the 1970's. The legendary movie hall shut down after a change of hands.

RIGHT: Rialto was just one of Mussoorie's six cinema halls. The advent of new technology like VCRs and home theatres pushed them to oblivion in the 1980s. (Picture Courtesy: Robert Hutchison)

From Bannu in the North West Frontier Province came Taneja with his well-worn Rolicord to leave behind images of the hill folk from the adjoining hills. He took the first colour print of 'Babu'—his friend Saran Lal Kapoor of the Remington Typewriter Company, and half the town flocked to see the miracle of a coloured print when it came back after processing in Bombay!

Now you do not have to go all the way to the big city, for, just below Christ Church is Melaram & Sons, the largest processing lab in town.

Das Studio near the Rialto Cinema (Rialto Gate) has vanished as has Rajpal Studio, which specialised in sepia-tone portraits at Picture Palace. As colour photography well and truly arrived in the 1970s, we had the late Gurmeet Thukral's robust body of work. We all miss you Gurmeet, for your imperishable images. Why did you have to go away without saying goodbye?

The Library Bazaar: a glazed albumen print (circa 1880) by the pioneer photographer TA Rust, shows the uncluttered Savoy Hotel end of Library.

But I have to admit that the Rusts have yet to find their rightful place. Ah! What would one do without their enchanting sepia-tones of a time when the bungalows were simply lime and mortar pasted on to four-anna bricks, topped with thatch roofs!

It is the landscapes of Landour and Mussoorie by Rust that speak louder than words. The story of my collection of old pictures of Landour and Mussoorie dates back to the 1970s. I can still hear the voices ringing in my ears: 'Wouldn't it be great to get hold of some old postcards of Mussoorie!' exclaimed my friend, author Ruskin Bond.

Of course! I knew it would. But it was easier said than done. Where would one start? .

'Great idea!' I muttered, convinced that this was a pipe dream.

Where on earth would one hunt for those elusive pictures? Hadn't the old colonials packed up and 'gone home'? Even the old kabariwallas turned into second-hand dealers, had become antique-dealers. They had no pictures.

Dragging my feet, I scoured the bazaar, walking into old Ram Swarup, whose Glamour Studio had given up its soul with the advent of colour photography. Trouble was while he had lots of old portraits; he had no old pictures of the town. Garrulously he remembered how he had once been elected a member of the Mussoorie Municipal Board.

'Yes! Yes!' I said irritably, 'But what does that have to do with old pictures?'

The last laugh was on me!

He remembered having seen some sepia-toned pictures in the Committee Room. However, by the time I got there, they were all gone, each single one of them. Stumped, I chatted with the storekeeper about the old days—those magical images of a bygone period. Could he help? Or at least point me in the right direction?

'There is a lot of junk lying around in the godown,' he said, pointing me in the general direction of a musty room where the debris of more than a century and a half lay.

'Help yourself. Be my guest!' he said teasingly, before losing himself in a pile of old records.

Lost, I too was peering under a pile of rusty galvanised-iron sheets; I pried deeper, and soon struck gold. Of course the frames had long ago succumbed to the mighty onslaught of a hundred monsoons. From these I was able to rescue, from certain oblivion, the last few plates of the celebrated photographer of the 1880s, TA Rust. The rest, as they say, was easy, as friends, acquaintances, collectors and photographers from all over the world sent in old pictures of our little Himalayan hill station as it used to be in the 19th century.

'When I came to Mussoorie in the 1960s,' reminisces author Ruskin Bond, 'my landlady, Miss Bean, was then in her late eighties. She told me that she remembered TA Rust was a very helpful person, always going that extra mile to help other folk.'

Those early days of photography were hazardous. According to the Mussoorie Miscellany, published in the 1920s, a certain Captain Charles Henry Deane Spread, of the Invalid Establishment, Landour, was struck by lightning and killed at Balahissar on September 3rd, 1879. He was preparing to develop some photographic plates and, in a heavy shower was collecting rainwater for the process from the guttering, when he was struck dead.

Rust copyrighted his pictures by scratching his name on the negatives. Much as I tried, long and hard, I found no leads on him. I left it at that. Maybe it was best that way or so I consoled myself. For his images had already triumphed over Time!

Later on, his son Julian Rust inherited the studio on Camel's Back Road. The late Princess Sita of Kapurthala, who came to St Helens Cottage, just above the Chateau, in the 1920s, told me that she remembered his little daughter, who he always brought along to social gatherings, dressed like a doll!

I let the story about the little girl dressed like a doll pass. What relevance did it have today? I said to myself.

Thirty years later, it all fell into place. I literally bumped into author Charlotte Cory at the Writers Bar in the Savoy Hotel. She had with

her a diary belonging to a family from Sri Lanka who had come out to Mussoorie in the 1860s.

'Have you heard of anyone called TA Rust?' she asked, settling down to a sun-downer.

What! You could have knocked me over with a feather!

It turned out that TA Rust came out from Ceylon and then moved on to Mussoorie. In those days of photography in its infancy, he took to the new technology like a fish to water, like all young people down the ages. His images of the rich and famous brought him instant recognition and fame and soon he was a man of considerable means.

Plays, fancy dress balls and theatre groups like the Mussoorie Theatre Group were very popular up until the 1930s.

Photography did not take long to reach colonial India. Barely a year after Monsieur Louis Jacques Mande Daguerre invented the daguerreotype process of photography with his 'heliographic pictures' in 1839, youngsters all over India took to this revolutionary technique. But it was an uphill struggle to capture faces and trees and scenery. Photographers had to ensure that their subjects posed and stayed still.

I stumbled upon more of Rust's pictures, from the turn of the century, in an album lying on the table of the Principal's office in St George's College, Barlowganj. The faded gold lettering of the dedication caught my eye: 'Presented to Rev Bro JF Byrne, OSP Principal of St. Fidelis School, Mussoorie. By the Masters and Pupils, as a token of their Esteem. 30th September 1902.'

How did it happen to be there on the table just at that very moment? I have always had the eerie feeling that one of the Rusts wanted me to find copies of their work. Or were it a ghostly spirit of old shutterbugs pulling me there? Or is this serendipity? Who knows?

Apparently, the album had just been brought all the way from Ireland—from the Patrician Brothers Monastery—for the school's 150 year celebrations. And then it was going back to the cold vaults again!

When I mentioned this father and son team of the Rusts to the late Miss Edith Garlah, who lived in Woodlands near the Clock Tower and passed away recently, she remembered Julian Rust for another reason altogether—he was an apiarist! 'Ah! He used to flavour his honey with vanilla!' she reminisces, smacking her lips adding: 'He would add a few drops of essence to the sugary syrup he had concocted for the bees to survive through the lean winter months when there were no flowers.'

Did Julian learn a thing or two from the bees about stinging? I do not know but I am told he was a flourishing photographer, who displayed his works by the roadside as so many of that trade did in those days. Apparently, he had a tiff with the City Fathers about the location of his stall. And bite back he did. One day, among his exhibits there appeared the beautifully executed likeness of the Chairman of the local Board,

PREVIOUS PAGES (80-81): 'In a hundred ages of the Gods, I could not tell thee of the glories of the Himalayas', SKAND PURANA.

mounted on an ass. It was not a genuine photograph but just a clever piece of artistry and fireworks followed.

Later, Julian sold off the family's photography business and went off to South Africa with his beautiful irish wife, Elizabeth Anne Nelligan. He had four children: Cecil, Violet, Helen and another who succumbed to diphtheria as an infant. The money vanished and his little daughter Helen, born in the summer of 1914, the one he always dressed up like a doll, today lives in humble circumstances, in what she refers to as 'the old cowshed'—their sprawling Mount Franion Estate, a few miles from Kandy, Sri Lanka. The three Rusts never married, Cecil, proprietary planter, traveller and Chairman of the Times of Ceylon, died in Westminster in 1960, aged 55. Violet too passed away in 1974. Her sisters' passing away had a profound effect on Helen. She lived on in the charming bungalow but the light had gone out in her life. In 1982, she sold the bungalow, a decision she bitterly regrets.

But Helen Rust, though slightly hazy of memory, battered by time, goes into the sunset with a blithe spirit and an unfailing faith in God. 'He looks after me,' she tells her visitors. 'I have no troubles.' Flipping over the pages of the family Bible, one notices the family crest emblazoned across it: *'Fortis et Stabilis!'* Yes! The brave and steadfast—that is how Helen Rust has lived her life. 'When I saw her last, she was in her 80s, still loves to pose as she talks! Yes! That is definitely your doll,' said Catherine emphatically.

Apart from that interlude, I guess it is these images of Landour and Mussoorie that speak louder than words. They tell their own story of a laidback lifestyle when

Miss Edith Garlah, one of the oldest residents of Mussoorie, passed away peacefully, just a few days short of her 100th birthday (last winter). Her family owned Woodland School in the 1960s.

The old hand-pulled rickshaws are gone with the changing times.

the Queen of Hills had not yet been ravaged by developers. The *memsahib* (madam) in a rickshaw, the virgin hillsides untouched by later-day settlers, the Mall—less peopled than it is today, they bring alive the mirth and gaiety, the laughter and the chatter, the life of the people long gone to rest and literally dug out from debris. Such was life in a small hill station: everyone knew everyone's little oddities and eccentricities, those quirks in human nature that make one so different, and yet so special. And these photographs tell their tale, dusted from antiquity.

To me they remain quintessential nostalgia—a visual proof of a 100 years of the camera in Mussoorie. They continue to defy the relentless march of 'Time' in these first foothills of the Garhwal Himalaya. 🪶

Some of Our Schools

By 1884, before the days of fun and frolic, Mussoorie had become 'the Edinburgh of the East' or a centre of European education, a vast seminary. From their very beginning, the English saw hill stations as refuges for European public school education for those who could not go back to England for getting a proper education. The salubrious clime and easy accessibility made Mussoorie an attractive place for the education of children who could not afford to go to British boarding schools.

Mussoorie's first school was Mr John MacKinnon's Mussoorie Seminary. By 1840, the Mussoorie Seminary boasted nearly 100 boarders and according to an old school brochure, 'of the best families in Northern India—to many of whom a sufficient education is here afforded, the plains of Hindustan being the field of their future fortunes.' The object of these schools was to give the sons and daughters of the Company's employees, a sound education at the lowest possible cost, and, as far as possible on the lines of schools in England. The senior masters and mistresses were imported from England to ensure that nothing was left undone to turn out pupils, physically and morally, as close to those brought up in the United Kingdom.

While other hill stations had one or two good schools, or even three well-known ones, Mussoorie always had a plethora of schools—like mushrooms they sprouted, some flourished, others vanished. Gone is

Maddock's School situated on what were to become the grounds of the Savoy Hotel at the turn of the century. This school was started by Reverend RM Maddock, the then Chaplain of Mussoorie, who sent for his brother from England to lend a helping hand in running the School.

The next local school to open was the Convent of Jesus and Mary, Waverley, that was started in 1845. Begum Samru of Sardhana, converted to Catholicism and built the famous Church at Sardhana near Meerut. She made quite a name for herself when she donated this property to the school. It had its formal opening on 18 September. Waverley was the second school to be established in India by the religious society of the Congregation of Jesus and Mary. It was the first of the Convent boarding schools in the Northern provinces. Waverley became a first class boarding school, chiefly for the daughters of officers. The first community consisted of five nuns of whom Mother Gonzaga was the Superior, and they arrived from Dehradun in bullock carts—a very different mode of transport from our comfortable school van! Through the years, it was necessary to make changes and additions to the buildings as the original ones were almost completely destroyed in the great earthquake of 1905. The different Superiors made further additions and improvements as the years went by.

Caineville School for girls was opened in 1865 by Archdeacon Pratt on the densely wooded 60 acre spread of the defunct Mussoorie School with only four pupils. Two years later there were 56 pupils on the books.

Around 1876-77, Hampton Court School was started as a strictly undenominational institution. This school is splendidly situated—the estate bordering the Mall and facing the south, with beautiful grounds and large buildings. In 1895, it was bought over by Miss Holland and thereafter it was known as Miss Holland's School. Miss Holland, the first Latin MA of the Bengal University, won the Roychand Premchand Grant and coming to Mussoorie, started a school at Arundel. She bought Hampton Court the next year. Very soon, the locals began to call it the

PREVIOUS PAGE: Woodstock School flag hoisting on Independence Day.

FACING PAGE: Reverend Maddock was the Chaplain of Mussoorie, who had his brother come out from England and start Maddock's School on a ridge above the Library Bazaar on what would at the turn of the 19th century become the site of the Savoy Hotel. (Picture Courtesy: Robert Hutchison)

'Calcuttiya School'. In 1922, the nuns of Jesus and Mary took over it, and further additions and improvements were made by the different Superiors as the years went by. Today, it is run as a day school from class pre-primary to 10th.

Another old school in Mussoorie, Wynberg-Allen, was founded more than a 100 years ago when a few public-spirited friends, led by Mr and Mrs Arthur Foy, Brigadier Condon and Mr Alfred Powell, got together in Kanpur to discuss how to best meet the needs of poor and orphan children of European and Anglo-Indian communities of Northern India. From this meeting emerged the idea of an orphanage-cum-training-centre run on Christian non-sectarian principles. The school started in 1886, in a very small way with just six pupils, in Rockville—one of Mussoorie's oldest buildings situated near Jabbarkhet on a hill a few kilometres out of Mussoorie. The headmistress Mrs Barton West took no salary and spent the rest of her life in improving the school and its standards. Under the building, was a charcoal kiln that burst one day and the school burnt out without any injuries to anyone. Today, this building is called the Haunted House. The institution was moved to 'Abbotsford' and 'Dunedin' on the Castle Hill Estate, and was eventually opened on its present site which is Balahissar in March 1894. The Wynberg-Allen Homes were a purely philanthropic undertaking when the main building with 'Constantia Hall', was burnt down in the late 1890s. Incendiarism was suspected. Then again, the same hall suffered badly in the earthquake of 1905. As Wynberg Estate once used to be the Masuri Hotel of which Mr Bobby Hesseltine was proprietor, it was often referred to as 'Bobby Sahib ka school' (Bobby Sahib's school) in the 1930s. The institution gradually acquired more students and staff and with the help of generous donations, was able to purchase the old Bobby's Hotel or the Wynberg Estate, overlooking the Doon Valley and the Siwalik Hills on the road to Rajpur and Dehradun. The school celebrated its centenary in 1988 and relived memories of past glory. It has a strength of 800 students.

The East India Railway School was in place at Oak Grove in 1888. With its 165 acres in Jharipani, it is land-wise certainly one of the largest schools in the hill station. It was, and still remains to be a school catering mostly to the children of Railway employees.

An interesting story attached to this school is that of one of its principals, who, was reputed to have found time for everything else but the administration of the school. One can safely say that probably, he was single-handedly responsible for the extinction of all wildlife in this area. From the crack of dawn, he would begin tracking down pheasants and then spend the afternoon splashing around in a bathtub. At dusk, in that magical hour of the cow-dust, he would be off again marauding the hillsides for game. He would never have got derailed but for his conspicuous absence once, during the school's annual day function. This modern-day Diogenes was still in his bath as the day's proceedings drew to a close. The Chief Guest, the *Hon'ble* Minister for Railways, was obviously not amused. Next day, reading the writing on the wall, the Principal put in his papers. When I last heard of him, he was hunting around in Dehradun looking for a new home with a Jacuzzi!

Of the Indian schools the Ghananand Inter College began in 1927 at Thespic Lodge behind the Landour Bazaar, moving to Kingcraig in 1928 where, though far from town, it continues to flourish. It is one of Mussoorie's oldest intermediate college and owes its origins to the philanthropy of the Khanduri family, wealthy timber contractors of Pauri Garhwal. With the wane in logging activities, the school went into a decline and in 1945, it was handed over to the government

The Arya Kanya Pathshala started in 1917 by B Ramchandra MWS, SDO, Landour, and after shifting several times found its present location at Kirkland Estate next to the Himalaya Club. Once upon a time, the old Kirkville Estate was known as 'Halim Castle' and the locals used to call it *Kuttakhana* or kennel, because, Mr Kirk used to keep a large pack of hunting dogs. Today, it has over 800 students and has made a name for itself in extra curricular activities and the National Cadet Corps training.

The Sanatan Dharam Inter College was started in 1928 opposite the Landour Temple and is run by the Sanatan Dharam Sabha.

In an act of educational philanthropy, two new schools were born, some 20 years ago: St Lawrence School (attached to Waverly Convent) and Nirmala School (supported by St Georges College) for the lesser fortunate sections of society.

The Indo-Tibetan Police's High Altitude Defence Survival Academy came up in the 1970s on the grounds of the old Caineville House. After many incarnations, it was the Shishu Niketan School before the ITBP (Indo-Tibetan Border Police) took over to train the various para military organisations in survival skills.

In the last 40 years, new schools have sprouted: Mussoorie Modern, Mussoorie Public, Mussoorie International, Guru Nanak Fifth Centenary. Though English medium education has always been in great demand in the hill station, the two Hindi Girl schools continue to prosper and have an excellent reputation. The Mussoorie Degree College serves the town and the surrounding area.

This listing of schools, lost and found, past and present, would be incomplete if one were to leave out the Lal Bahadur Shastri National Academy of Administration, which has for the last 50 years been instrumental in training officers of the All India Services. In 1958, the old Chajauli Estate, on which the Charleville was built, were taken over by the Government to house the national academy. So, it will be safe to assume that each and every officer of the All India Services has spent the spring of their lives attending the foundational course conducted here from August to December.

Some of the schools withered away and are almost forgotten today. Among these were Philander Smith School, which moved to Nainital, where it continues to flourish; the Junior Mussoorie School once in the Abbey; the Modern School of Bassett Hall; Mr Moore's Landour Boarding and Day School of Sunny Bank, and later Mullingar; and Mr Sheeshan's Academy where the Civil Hospital stands today.

Statue of Lal Bahadur Shastri at the National Academy of Administration.

Among Mussoorie's old schools, Vincent Hill School was perhaps the most unconventional. Organised and managed by the Seventh Day Adventist Mission, it was started in Annfield and later moved to the site of today's Guru Nanak Fifth Centenary. Although the curriculum was not dissimilar to that in most educational institutions, many of the students were trained for Holy Orders, or for colportage. Unlike other schools, it relied as little as possible on hired labour, and pupils were therefore given considerable training in household duties and developing manual skills. The excellent products from the school bakery, hawked around the station, were a living testimony of what the students were capable of in the culinary department. Indeed, the tradition of producing peanut butter in town has its origins in this school.

The schools were much more than just bread and butter for the teachers. Perhaps just being cooped-up in one place for nine months in a year was recipe enough for trouble: murders, suicides, intrigues and disappearances were the order of the day. When I mentioned this to my friend Ruskin Bond, he remembered his brief brush with schooling here.

LEFT: One of the last pictures of the Charleville Hotel before the main building was lost to a fire in the 1970s.

RIGHT: The office of the Charleville Hotel's Manager is a fine heritage building. It is the Director's Office at the Lal Bahadur Shastri National Academy of Administration.

On his first day at Convent of Jesus and Mary at Hampton Court: 'Off to school' did not always mean 'Off to study'. Ruskin reveals, 'Oh! It had nothing to do with reading and writing. It was terrible. I kicked and screamed. I think I even kicked the Reverend Mother on her shins! Perhaps one of the reasons I was never very popular with her.' Ruskin still remembers a boy he liked in school and with whom he used to share his desk. They had made plans to run away together. So, they would save their tuck—bits of bread, rusks, and other nibbles and, eventually, everything would become hard and mouldy.

Schools like these were really staging posts or waiting rooms for boys and girls going on to bigger schools. You took nothing away and you left nothing behind.

Interestingly, the tradition of running away from school continues. Even today, if you see two or three incongruous nuns at the fork of the Library peering into lines of taxis, surely the nuns are not looking for a lift! They must be looking for some of the girls from the Waverly Convent who have escaped into the wilds of the Doon valley and beyond!

Library Chowk is the focal point of all political rallies and flag-hoisting on Independence Day. This occasion marks a major celebration for school children.

Until 1947, it was rather easy to get admission in these hill schools. The Indian middle class had not yet bludgeoned and only the affluent Indians could afford admission. The ease with which you could get into schools, as compared to today when you would give an arm and a leg just to step through the gates, was amazing. My own experience is a case in point. Even though we were working class, when I went to school in the 1950s, I simply walked into the school near Balahissar and met the Principal, the genial Reverend WJ Biggs. He peered at me through his thick-rimmed spectacles balanced on his nose, looked me up and down, and said: 'Come from tomorrow! Uniform can come later!'

By the 1970s it was no longer this simple, people were queuing up outside the gates of the English medium schools! The rise of the middle class had begun.

Woodstock is one of the finest international schools in the station. Choosing Mussoorie because of its climate must have been an easy choice for the school's pioneers. Its humble origins can be traced back to 1854, when, four ladies from the 'London Society for Promoting Female Education in the East' landed in Calcutta and began the long journey up to Mussoorie. They had come in response to an appeal from a committee in Mussoorie consisting of three army officers, the Chaplain of Mussoorie and two American missionaries. Their aim was to start a Protestant Christian School of a quality equivalent to that of Waverley Convent. It opened in Caineville Estate but later moved to the other end of Mussoorie, to the Woodstock Estate, where it has been flourishing ever since. Colonel Reilly had constructed the house named Woodstock in 1842. In 1867, after Colonel Reilly's death, the school purchased the estate from his widow.

The estate adjacent to Woodstock, known as Midlands, was owned by Mr George Taylor of the East India Company, and after him is named the school's only playing ground. In the first decade of the 20th century, Woodstock School was expanding and a teacher's training college was added to the school. To accommodate the college, Woodstock

FOLLOWING PAGES (94-95): The older Mussoorie schools are perched atop spurs commanding stunning views of the Doon Valley down below. The Horse-shoe valley with the Woodstock School in the foreground and the Wynberg-Allen School and the St George's College on the two spurs down below.

purchased the Midlands Estate and expanded the old tumbled down building to house the college. The college building closed in 1935 and the building became the senior girls' hostel, Midlands, and that is what it is to this day.

Woodstock School at the end of 2008 had 485 pupils—all boarders —from 28 different nationalities and an international set of teachers. The school strives to retain a predominantly American character.

The school, straddles a ridge, spread over 260 acres, and has been providing distinctive education to students from 30 countries.

Only in 1926 did the school become co-educational and the colourful school brochure says:

> 'Living at Woodstock can be an adventure. Some students from less-developed countries regard the facilities as luxurious. Some from developed countries regard them as Spartan. That is Woodstock in a nutshell. It teaches resourcefulness. It builds life-long relationships. It bridges worlds.'

Ruskin Bond at Cambridge Book Depot for a book-signing session.

Among the many things in its varied curriculum, is the 'Activity Week' in the fall. The entire student body moves out of the classrooms and heads for the outdoors. This is the time for them to indulge in their chosen avocation—hiking, biking, rafting, or maybe a historical or cultural tour. Younger students remain close to home; explore the hillsides of Mussoorie and the valley of the Doon. High School students trek into the mighty Himalayan ranges, walk through the forts of Rajasthan or touch the ghats of Varanasi. The students are free to take their pick, under the watchful eye of a well-qualified

international faculty, drawn from far afield as Australia, North America, and Europe.

Saturdays are usually days when the students go down to old Landour Bazaar. On this day, the aroma of fresh food permeates the bazaar. Tibetan dumplings called *momos*, butter chicken, hot breads called *naan*, sweetmeats like *jalebi* and fire-roasted corn-cobs rubbed with lime juice and salt. Indeed the association between the bazaar and Woodstock go back over a 100 years. The shopkeepers are familiar with the students and share an affectionate bond with them.

Another special aspect of the school is life in the residences. Joyce Campbell, an old alumnus writes:

> 'As a child I was brought up in India, my father being in the Indian Army, I was fortunate to have been a student of Woodstock School during the Second World War. It was one of the happiest times of my life. I am still in contact with various members of my class and recently met up with two of them living in the west of England—after 22 years! The years just peeled away and it was like yesterday, we were girls again—this is thanks to the magic of Woodstock…'

Some of the school buildings are older than the school. Most of these are homes for the staff living on campus. But there are newer structures like the Media Centre with three computer labs—one exclusively dedicated to journalism, an auditorium, a world-class gymnasium, a spacious art studio, a video-editing suite and a screening room. At the time of writing, the school forges ahead to keep pace with other international schools, scattered all over the world. Woodstock has kept pace with the Sandman, constantly reinventing itself, changing with the times and as Sanjay Narang,

Woodstock School's legendary music department has consistently brought laurels to the school across the years.

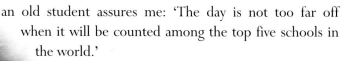

an old student assures me: 'The day is not too far off when it will be counted among the top five schools in the world.'

At the other end of the economic divide, are the lesser fortunate ones who have to trudge to the vernacular day schools. A day in their lives begins on a dark, sultry monsoon morning, when a 16-year-old Pushpa Singh opens the doors of her home in the Park Estate, to see a perfect white out. But she knew pretty well what the clouds hid, for, whenever they parted, she would once again see a perfect view of the snow-capped peaks of the Himalayas—peak after peak rising to touch the skies.

'Must not forget to take the umbrella today,' she muttered to herself. Yes! School was a long walk from home. The hunger for learning makes many children walk eight kilometres to school one-way and there is no one who can take chances with predicting the fickle weather in the hills, where, one minute it might be sunshine, and, the next you find yourself in the middle of a cold thunderstorm.

On the roof of her humble home were chattering monkeys, and wisps of mist rose in the valley stretching out before her. Her father was the night watchman of the old property, the Park Estate, till he passed away. Now she lives with her uncle who is working in her father's position. She loves walking to school along the long narrow path over the ridge covered with the wild kingora bushes, full of sweet berries, and to ford the little rivulets cascading from springs on the hillsides.

In these hills, there are myriad boulder-strewn rivers and villages and one finds chequered a few lonely dwellings like the one Pushpa and many others like her live in. Her father, like other cultivators in the hills, was poor. Nevertheless, these poor cultivators are sturdy human beings

The hunger for learning fills up the kindergartens of vernacular schools like Mussoorie Girls Inter College, with children from local homes who can ill-afford the exhorbitant fee of the English medium schools.

and display wonderful powers of endurance. They manage to wrest a precarious living from the unhelpful calcinated soil of the region.

Medical facilities, however, are sometimes hard to come by. The sick have to walk (if they can!) or be carried great distances to reach a functioning hospital. At times, the ailing simply stays at home until they get better or fail to get better.

Many roads are either mule tracks or footpaths and, although in more than 60 years of Independence, new roads have opened up several remote areas, large tracts of the region cannot be reached, except on foot. So, sometimes letters from someone living in say Mussoorie, may take one to three weeks to reach his village, though, as the crow flies, the distance may not be any more than 50 miles.

Yet, the hill folk, paradoxically, are the most contented of people. There is enough to get by on and the unyielding fields provide solace if not enough food.

Children attending school from the nearby villages.

Pushpa's favourite game as she walks to school in the serenity of the hills is to spot birds. I ask her for her favourite bird. 'Oh! The bamboo partridge has no peers', she says, adding, 'it always seems to trumpet a challenge to an imaginary hunter to pursue it to its inaccessible home.' So confident is it of its own security, its war-song does not cease. Nature is on its side for it has given the bamboo partridge a plumage that is in perfect harmony with the habitat. Only sometimes, has Pushpa managed to creep up to its nest and give it a real surprise!

But her school is no surprise for Pushpa. Predictably, it is not made of shimmering granite, steel and glass. The Mussoorie Girls School was started in the summer of 1917 by a philanthropist and after shifting location several times, it was finally relocated to the present Kirkland Estate below the old Himalaya Club.

Spread over five acres, the school building is still the way the early pioneers built them. Old houses like these sit comfortably on the hillsides under whispering pines and tell a tale all of their own—but they will not reveal their secrets easily! Only the chosen ones, who can wait and listen, learn all.

Those Who Never Went Home

Sir C Farrington, Bart, lies near the spot he died. This was by the side of the Rajpur-Mussoorie bridle path, to the left of Halfway House. Maybe he was too ill to make it to the Convalescent Depot and died enroute to be buried here. The original grave was lost in a landslide but a replica was re-erected later near the spot.

There were some who were going to be here with us forever—those who sleep eternally under the crosses that dot the eastern slope of Landour and the north face of Camel's Back. These are our very own villages of silence where vandalism has forced the Cemetery Committees to padlock the gates in these prosaic times, otherwise for the diligent seeker, a lavish store of knowledge lies in a quiet walk through the cemeteries. Jharipani is home to a monolith for the first European who did not go home—Sir C Farrington, Bart, of the 35th Regiment, who died on March 28th, 1828, aged 35 years. Perhaps he was ill and came up to recuperate in the Invalids Depot in Landour. His grave is still there by the side of the old bridle road, near Halfway House in Jharipani. This is the first recorded death in these hills.

Around the Upper Mall in Landour, you could tarry a while before the earthly haven of Captain George Bolton, one of the earliest graves here. The simple epitaph says it all:

'Sacred to the memory of Captain George Bolton, HC's (Honourable Company's) 2nd European Regiment, who after months of painful suffering, departed this life on 13th June in the year of our Lord 1828.

AGED 40.
His virtuous and amiable disposition rendered him
Generally beloved in life and lamented in death.
This memorial is erected by his affectionate widow.'

Not many know that among those sleeping on the Camel's Back Cemetery is one of Balaclava's immortal six hundred—John Hindmarsh. He was laid to rest by only two men—Mr JC Fisher and Mr HE Hathaway—both of who later declared that they would have marshalled the whole station to pay final tribute to this gallant survivor of 'The Charge of the Light Brigade'. If you look up the history books, you will find that during the Crimean War in 1854, at Balaclava, a misinterpreted command led to the cream of the British cavalry to charge into certain death under the boom of the Russian guns. Just a 100 survived the 'Charge of the Light Brigade'. What could John Hindmarsh possibly have been doing up in the hills? There is no one to tell now. His inscription tells us that he was 'One of the Six Hundred'.

PAGE 101: Ruskin Bond, Mussoorie's famed author in residence, rediscovered the grave of Australian author, John Lang in the Camel's Back Cemetery in the 1970s.

BELOW: The lych-gate of the Camel's Back Cemetery is just one of the hill station's structures that still remain the same.

It was warriors like Hindmarsh who Alfred Tennyson, the Victorian Poet Laureate, had in mind when he wrote:

> Cannon to the right of them,
> Cannon to the left of them,
> Cannon behind them,
> Volleyed and thundere'd;
> Storm'd at with shot and shell,
> While horse and hero fell,
> They that had fought so well,
> Came thro' the jaws of Death,
> Back from the mouth of Hell,
> All that was left of them,
> Left of the six hundred.

After the battle, Hindmarsh moved to India with his regiment and was simply recuperating in the hills where he finally came to rest in the solitude of this quiet corner of Mussoorie. His wife lies buried beside him.

Also finding a resting place at the Camel's Back Cemetery are Pahari Wilson and his wife Gulabi. To be buried in consecrated ground, Gulabi was baptised 'Ruth'. You cannot leave this cemetery without paying respect to John Lang, the first Australian born author, who

BELOW: Raja Pahari Wilson and his wife Gulabi's grave are on the first terrace below the lych-gate of the Camel's Back Cemetery. (Picture Courtesy: Robert Hutchison)

BELOW RIGHT: Pahari Wilson's tombstone.

FACING PAGE TOP: Plaque under a strapping 60 foot cypress tree was planted in 1870 by HRH Duke of Edinburgh on a visit to the Landour Cemetery

FACING PAGE BELOW: A plaque on the tomb of John Lang.

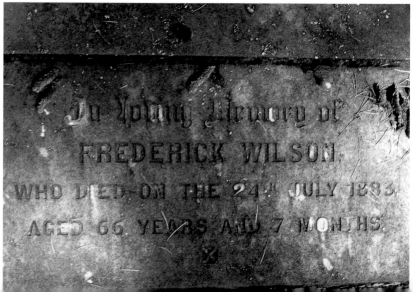

In loving memory of
FREDERICK WILSON,
WHO DIED ON THE 24th JULY 1883,
AGED 66 YEARS AND 7 MONTHS.

left Calcutta for Meerut, and spent the last years of his life in Landour. He was a maverick, a gifted one at that, who was forced out of Australia in his youth for his anti-establishment views. Arriving in India, he defended the Rani of Jhansi in her litigation with the John Company just before the Mutiny. She rewarded him well—a thousand guineas, besides such presents as shawls, dresses, ornaments and a mosaic portrait of the Rani in precious stones. What have outlived him are his early Australian novels—*The Forger's Wife, Botany Bay*. It seems the novels of the Indian period, *Too Clever By Half* and *Too Much Alike* published in London in 1853 and 1854 respectively, have been

The haunting lilt of bagpiper pays tribute to fallen soldiers in the Landour Cemetery.

unfairly neglected. They painted a satirical picture of the British period in India, which did not go down too well with the die-hards of the British Raj.

Another forgotten cemetery that lies tucked away below the Landour Cemetery is the Roman Catholic one. In it are interred the remains of the Italian prisoners-of-war who passed away during their internment at the time of the Second World War. However, no granite, marble or handsome mausoleums have been built over them. They are shaped like chimneys made of ordinary slate with mortar and pestle. Nevertheless, while the grander ones have crumbled to dust, these indigenous tributes have withstood the test of time and serve as a remembrance, of a period in our not too ancient history.

These and many more are gentle reminders that men and their matters perish. Only the mountains are there forever.

Mussoorie's Newspapers

The Mussoorie Times

WITH WHICH ARE INCORPORATED

THE MAFASILITE, THE HILL ADVERTISER, THE HIMALAYA CHRONICLE, AND THE ECHO.

Published at the MAFASILITE PRINTING WORKS, MUSSOORIE, U.P.A. & O.

No. 25.

Vol. XXXVI.

MUSSOORIE, FRIDAY, JUNE 19, 1936.

Addresses

Get your eyes tested for the cure of headaches, watering and redness of eyes and weak sight

WEST END OPTICAL Company,
West End House, Kulri.

Protect your eyes with genuine Crooke's Glasses.
Use Zeiss Lenses for Reading.
Also call for choicest frames, lenses, cases etc..

Telephone No. 51.

T.F.O.

Dr. S. KOPELIOWITCH,
M. D. (BERLIN),
MEDICAL COUNCILLOR (VIENNA),
Latest Shock-proof X-Ray Plant for diagnostic and deep treatment. Short and long-wave diathermy etc.

Hakman's Grand Hotel
Room No. 30.

Phone No. 43.

16-10-36.

Dr. W. C. CARPER
D.D.S., F.I.C.D., F.A.D.S.
Dental Surgeon,
Cronstadt House,
THE MALL,
Phone 709.

30-10-36.

International Dental Surgeon
Dr. N. N. BERY
D.D.S. (PENN U.S.A.) D.E.D.P. (PARIS,)
Z.D.S., Z.O.S. (VIENNA)
Late Dental Surgeon in Lyon, Vienna and Prague.

Winter: Queensway New Delhi.
ELLESMERE HOUSE
THE MALL, TEL. 30.

T.F.O.

Pindi Dass of M|S Pindi Dass & Co.
LAHORE, LUCKNOW, DELHI.
Chief Life and Fire Agents for U.P. and Punjab.

Communicate for the present at,
HAZEL BRAE
(Burjwali,) Mussoorie, U.P.

P—19-9-36.

Church Notices

CHRIST CHURCH.
MUSSOORIE.

Sunday, 21st June 1936.

SECOND AFTER TRINITY.

Holy Communion   8-00 a.m.
Children's Service   10-00 a.m.
Matins and Sermon   11-00 a.m.

ST. EMILIAN'S
(Church of the Sacred Heart)

Friday 19th June 1936
Feast of the Sacred Heart—Mass at 7-30 a.m.
"   "   The Holy
"   "   Hour from 6 to 7 p.m.
Sunday 21st June
Pontifical Mass by Bishop Vanni at 8-30.

The Choir will be supplied by the girls of the Waverley Convent.
Procession of the Blessed Sacrament in the Church compound at 6 p.m.

CONVENT CHAPEL

Sunday Mass   8 o'clock
Rosary and Benediction   5 o'clock
Week Days Mass   7 o'clock

CHURCH OF THE RESURRECTION
Barlowganj.

Holy Communion and Sermon 11-00 a.m.
Preacher – Revd. F. W. Hawke
Evensong and Sermon   6-00 p.m.
Preacher :- Mr. K.F. MacGowan

ALL SAINT'S CHURCH,
Castle Hill Estate.
No Service this week

HOOPER MEMORIAL CHAPEL.
Happy Valley.
Holy Communion (English)   8-00 a.m.
Hindustani Service   5-30 p.m.

KELLOGG MEMORIAL CHURCH,
Landour.

Junior Church   9.45 a.m.
Morning Service   11-00 a.m.
Hindustani Service   12-30 noon
Evening Service   5-00 p.m.
Prayer Service—held weekly on Thursday evenings at 5 p.m.

UNION CHURCH.

Sunday June 21st 1936.
Morning Service   11 a.m.
(For boys and girls and young people)
Evening Service   5-30 p.m.
Wednesday June 24th
Prayer Meeting (in vestry)   6 p.m.
Thursday June 25th
United Bible Fellowship   5-30 p.m.
Speaker, N. J. Everard Esq. F.R.C.S., L.R.C.P. M.R.C.S.

Saturday June 27th   9 p.m.
Lantern Lecture
Subject: Tutankhaoam and the
Treasurers of His Tomb
Lecture: Rev. G.P. Tasker of Bangalore
— All are cordially invited —

THE METHODIST EPISCOPAL CHURCH.
Kulri.

Sunday School   10-30 a.m.
Hindustani Service   12 noon
English Service   5-30 p.m.
Preacher Rev. R. 1. Faucett.

Wednesday Prayer Meeting   6-00 p.m.
Thursday United Bible Fellowship   5-30 p.m.
in the Union Church.

The Mussoorie Times

FRIDAY, JUNE 19, 1936.

News and Notes.

We start this week's notes with another appeal which we trust will not go altogether unheeded. The All-India Olympic Association requires Rs. 500 from this province for the expenses of the team going overseas. The sum was wanted by the 15th but Mr. Bhatty, U. P. General Secretary for the branch has promised to send whatever he can collect by June 26. In this behalf he issues an appeal for donations, each of which will be acknowledged. Mr. Jha and Col. Bell are amongst the earliest subscribers and we hope hundreds will follow, even if they cannot give more than eight annas. Donations should be sent Mr. Bhatty, "Clover Bank", Landour.

It will be recalled that Mr. Rashid Anwar who wrestled here in last year's Olympic games was the first Indian to notch a point for India in the sphere of sport overseas. This was at the British Empire Games at London in 1934. It is desired to send him with the team now going out to represent India, but unless this Rs. 500 is received by June 26 that desire will be unfulfilled. In the same cause is a dance being held after the final of the Mussoorie Olympic meet at the Rink on Friday 26. There certainly is no lack of dancers here and if these would support the function in full measure it will help considerably.

Also for the same purpose there is to be an exhibition hockey match at Taylor's Flat to-morrow, at 5 o'clock, St. George's College playing 'The Rest', for which admission is eight annas for adults and four annas for the schools and all other children.

With the strong executive that the Mussoorie Sports Association now has there is no further doubt about local sport being made a big feature of each season's activities — provided sportsmen support the games adequately. That the games which start next Monday at the Rink are not "exactly in your line" is, we feel, insufficient excuse for any sportsman not giving this inauguration his blessing by his presence, at least, if not by his entry. Begun at this season there just cannot be additions to the programme or there would have been, but it really is true that these games are to be spread over the whole season from next year, so do please encourage the executive to further efforts by showing that you have some little interest in their first undertaking.

We have been asked to announce that there is to be a sale of very handsome, darned, net lace, at 'The Priory', next Thursday from 2 p.m. This is a cottage industry of Dummagudem in South India. Prices at the sale will range from six annas to Rs. 40.

If you, who complain that there is little out of the ordinary at Mussoorie in the sphere of entertainment, will go to the Landour Amateur Dramatic Club's performance to-morrow evening at the Rink, of Jerome K. Jerome's "The passing of the third floor back", we can assure you that you will find that something different you are in search of. Apart from the pleasure you will, we hope, derive from seeing this unusual play, you will help the Cottage Hospital and the Community Hospital to aid which the play is being presented.

In the coming week's programme do not overlook the King's birthday celebrations: two specially planned entertainments at the Palladium next Tuesday; and the 'Argentina' night at the Savoy on

---

NOTICE

*N*ewspapers have always had a place of pride in the hill station. It is a tradition we owe to John MacKinnon, who started off the race with the publication of *The Hills* in 1842, but by 1840, it died out, only to be resurrected in 1865 and perish once again.

The Mussoorie Exchange Advertiser was exactly what the name suggests, just a broadsheet advertising of all sorts of establishments and their wares. A look at those advertisements reveal a lot about what was really happening in the early days of life in Mussoorie. Of course, a student of history will notice that for the first time, the old 'Masuri' was transforming into the modern 'Mussoorie'.

In 1875, John Northam published *The Himalaya Chronicle* but we remember him today for bringing out the first proper guide of the hills in 1884. His *Guide to Masuri, Landaur, Dehradun & the Hills North of Dehra* is a comprehensive compendium of lives and the paths it took in those early days. No book on our little hill station can ever be written without reference to this lodestone.

'The following pages cannot pretend to much originality,' complained F Bodycot, owner of the Mafasilite Printing Works in 1907, as he wrote the next best *Guide to Mussoorie*. Harold C Williams, Editor of the Mafasilite Press, who as the anonymous Rambler authored the gossipy *Mussoorie Miscellany* in 1931. Its doggerel, classic understatement and tongue-in-cheek style continues to charm the reader even today.

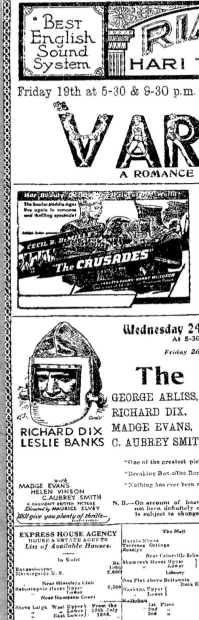

The Mussoorie Times

WITH WHICH ARE INCORPORATED

THE MAFASILITE, THE HILL ADVERTISER, HIMALAYA CHRONICLE, and THE ECHO.

VOL. XXXVI. No. 25.   MUSSOORIE, FRIDAY, JUNE 19, 1936.   PRICE ONE ANNA

I feel the tradition of small town newspapers carries on to this day—there are over 386 newspapers, big and small, registered in the Doon, at the end of 2008!

Old newspapers like the *Mussoorie Times*, kept a record of the rise and fall of the hill station. We find, that by the turn of the century, the special magic of the hills had begun to vanish. The trouble-plagued schools floundered: Caineville perished, Bramleigh Towers wound-up while others managed to stem the tide.

The Years of Decline

After the bridle path, another road to Mussoorie was slowly snaking its way up the hill. The Cart Road by-passed the old Rajpur Road and by 1920, Colonel EW Bell, Swetenham's son-in-law, drove the first car, a T-model Ford up to the Fitch & Co (today's Railway Out Agency) on the Mall in Kulri. In 1926, the road had crept up to Bhatta, and in 1930 up to Sunny Views, and in 1936 it had reached the terminus in Kincraig. Soon the Scindia-owned Gwalior and Northern India Transport Co Ltd was plying its buses from Saharanpur. Trouble was the heavy bullock and horse traffic left animal shoes and nails littered all over it. Labour contracts were given out for clearing the road of these offending impediments to the smooth flow of rubber wheels.

Mussoorie and Landour had become a Garden of Eden where the British had turned the world they found into a world they wished it to be. All around the hillsides, they discovered the common English wildflowers that were reminiscent of the hills and dales of England. Masses of sweet peas, geraniums, fuchsias, lilies, dahlias, soon bedecked the hill cottages while garden escapees graced the precipitous slopes. It was these flower-bedecked homes that were sprinkled over the hillsides and in the swirling mist one could almost 'feel' one was 'back home' in old Blighty!

There was a brief upward turn in fortunes in the 1920s but then came the slump. The District Gazetteer of 1934 paints a dismal picture:

PREVIOUS PAGE: Heavy snowfalls like this one are getting rarer as the years go by. The last six-footer was in 1960 when it snowed all the way down till Rajpur at the foot of the hills. In times like these, God's frozen children head for the plains!

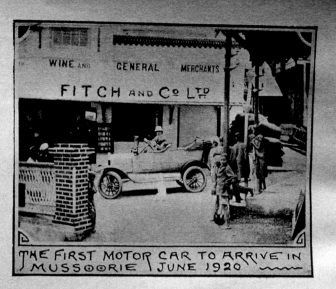

An early Motor arrival in - MUSSOORIE.

In the third week of June in the year 1920 a Ford Motor negotiated the cart road up to the Library for the first time in the history of the Station. To thoroughly test the suitability of the Ford Engine and the roads (so called) in the Station, the Car was driven over the roads between the Library, the Charleville Hotel, Herne Dale, around the Camels Back up Kulri Hill and down Fitch's Hill. All gradients met with were negotiated with ease, safety and without the least difficulty. The Car and its driver were equal to all emergencies.

The experiments demonstrated that Motor Traffic in the Station is possible or will become so when the roads have been widened and improved and some of the harp corners eased. The journey, up Hill from Rajpore occupied one hour, and assuming that the cart road was improved to suit Motor traffic, the journey from Dehra Dun to the Charleville should easily be done in that time.

THE FIRST MOTOR CAR TO ARRIVE IN MUSSOORIE JUNE 1920

39

'The Happy Valley Club is to be closed next year; the Race Course and Polo Ground have been derelict for some years; the Himalaya Club was closed even before 1920, as were the two breweries.'

But all was not black as black can be. Rescue came with the arrival of the Indian professionals: doctors, engineers, small landlords and successful businessmen stepped in to fill up the gap left by the departing Englishmen. They bought their properties, took over their cottage homes and put their children into the schools. Before one could blink, the place was entirely theirs.

In October 1929, Mahatma Gandhi came up to Mussoorie and held a prayer meeting on the Sylverton Flat. Here he was presented with a silver replica of a hill *dandi*—a modification of the palanquin carried by

The first car seen above reached Mussoorie in 1920, when, Col EW Bell drove a T-model Ford across the Mall to Clarence House where Fitch & Co had a shop.

four porters, which he auctioned on the spot for Rs 908. This amount went towards his Khadi Development Fund.

Post Independence, there were some who 'stayed on': the Wilkes sisters at Bellevue, the Buchanan sisters in Elcot Lodge, the Powells in Wayside Cottage, the Fosters in Maryville, the Garlah family— Cecil, Dorris and Edith in Woodlands. But one by one, they merged into the greyness of the changing times and were lost forever. Today, you have just the Skinners of the famous Skinner's Horse Regiment of the Indian Army, in Sikander Hall, Barlowganj, to remind us of those days of wine and roses.

The dark period of the 1960s in the station's history gets usually glossed over, but they were indeed very bad times. Old houses were remorselessly pulled down, cannibalised for stone, tin and timber. Gone are places like Dunsverick and Guthrie Lodge, (the once-imperial residences of the Maharaja of Baroda); Holly Mount (today home to the handsome business tycoon, Rajbir Handa); Wolfsburn (where

Crown Brewery in Barlowganj frames neighbouring Sikander Hall, home to the illustrious family of the Skinners.

Mrs Edith Walsh had a guest house in the 1960s and is now Professor Uniyal's home); Cosy Nook (once owned by the Tehri Raja and then home to the late Mrs Roberts of Hakmans); and the old Parsonage (near the Landour Cemetery and where actor Victor Banerjee now lives).

> Hark, hark the dogs shall bark,
>
> The beggars have come to town,
>
> Some in rags and some in bags,
>
> And some in velvet gowns...

This old nursery rhyme illustrates the road taken in the late 1980s by our homes in the hills. There are some, who feel that the tipping point was the troubles in Punjab post 1983 when these hills turned into a parking lot for black money. Everyone wanted a place to escape to in case things really got out of hand.

With the influx of funds, the point of no return had been crossed, and prices sky-rocketed—homes that cost a few thousand went into lakhs. Waterways and nullahs were filled up and built over. Property

BELOW LEFT: An old colonial bungalow above Masonic Lodge was briefly a Swedish School untill 1965. Today it's just another hotel in town.

BELOW: Up to the 1970s, almost every other home in the hill station had its own pet. With the advent of the flat-culture, pets are almost a thing of the past.

prices went through the roof and many old cottages were pulled down. In the beginning of the present slumification, the land developers trickled in peddling their dreams of 'flats' in the hills and in their wake came the builders. Together they were to change the face and nature of the hill station. Every little watershed sprouted apartments or multistoreyed hotels.

To pander to the mania of building flats upon flats and apartments upon apartments, private homes began to vanish—the Maharani of Jaipur's Liveland Estate, the Powell's Home at Seven Oaks and Wakefield Cottage.

On Camel's Back the face of the entire southern slope metamorphosi's hit old world homes like Rest Heaven and Tullamore. At the time of writing, I hear that the old Maryville Estate in Barlowganj is about to be pulled down.

Straddling a ridge facing the Doon Valley along the Kipling Road is the striking Antlers Cottage. Almost a 150 years later it continues to retain its unique character.

PREVIOUS PAGES (118-119): *Hanging on to the lip of the first foothills of the Himalayas, Mussoorie as seen from Chandal Garhi. 'Stand still for five minutes and they will build a hotel around you!' said an old Mussoorie resident. The old houses are now hidden behind the concrete monstrosities. Without paint, the tin-roofs look as if they have been made out of hammered out biscuit-tins. Today, the houses perched precariously on the lip of a ridge, huddle together as if for comfort.*

The dirge for lost homes is a song of nostalgia. It laments the loss of bungalow-styled Kenneth Lodge to pragmatic Mahajan Villa; wisteria-clad Catherine Villa to monolithic Jas Apartments; turreted Fairlawn Palace to pin-cushioned Kamal Towers; tin-roofed Heaven's Club to a characterless Shipra; brick-clad Madelsa House to a concrete Tibetan Nunnery; Kalsia Estate into Pearl Hotel & Shivam Hotel; Rock Cliffe to Avalon Resorts; tree-draped Arundale Cottage to deserted Priyank Apartments; oak-covered Sapling Estate to a building-block like MS Resorts; honey-suckle laden Rosemary Cottage to plastic-palmed Oasis Hotel; glamorous Glenhead to sullen Silver Rock; sprawling Sylverton Hotel to three hotels—Park Plaza, Dream Hotel and Tara Rudisson

The hall of Stephen and Amita Alter's home, Oakville, is a tribute to the early artisans craft in using just local lime and mortar to stunning effect. Stephen is Mussoorie's youngest author and his novels include 'Neglected Lives', 'Silk and Steel', 'The Godchild', 'All the Way to Heaven' and 'Renuka'. These novels are a tribute to his writing prowess. (Picture Courtesy: Stephen Alter)

LEFT: *On a flat carved out of a ridge above the Jharipani Ridge, Fairlawn Palace built by the deposed Ranas of Nepal in 1902, with some help from the Patrician Brothers of St Georges College.*

RIGHT: *Minus the hoardings, the Exchange Building is almost just as it was ninety years ago.*

Hotel; grand Himalaya Club to Himalaya Club and Himalaya Castle and silver-roofed Ashton Court to the space-age Hanifil Foundation.

Perhaps that was the way it had to be. Mussoorie came into prominence because of its easy accessibility and it was finally paying the price for being too close to the plains! 🪶

Landour Survives

$\mathcal{W}$hat survived of some cataclysmic changes in the hill station was the Landour Cantonment. Luckily, Landour was more or less undisturbed, because there was no space to build. The descendants of those early traders who followed the Redcoats from Meerut, Roorkee, Landuara, Thana Bhawan and Saharanpur were not interested in selling their shops to the newcomers. They were content to follow the peaceful tenor of their simple lives.

If you get here, find yourself a cozy nook, a glade, and a knoll—for this Cantonment spreads over some 1,070 acres with just 78 houses. Its quaint bazaar has 300 shops where you will find almost anything you require for your daily needs: dealers in fruits and vegetables, grain-merchants, and traders of all shapes and sizes.

Walking up the Mullingar slope, the ascent to Landour begins—shops on the right and houses (like Annandale, Eglantine and such) on the left, until you turn sharp to the east again under Trim Lodge. From here the different roads branch off; one to the left, going up past the old rickshaw stand. This is the shortest but steepest road up to the Church; the one to the right, going away on a much easier gradient leads on to Nag Tibba. From above here also branches off the Edge Hill Road and the main road to Tehri, passing under Woodstock School.

Having arrived at St Paul's Church one is near the middle of Landour. Southward and below lie a cluster of houses and three or four barracks;

some more private houses, the Roman Catholic Chapel of St Peter's, the two cemeteries and Childers Castle, Lodge and Cottages beyond the Cantonment northern boundary. Eastward lies Lal Tibba, more barracks, more private houses, and, towards the eastern boundary, the Institute of Technology Management. The highest point in Landour is the Roman Catholic Chapel, 7,850 ft above sea level; Lal Tibba is 7,464 ft; and both these towers some 1,500 ft over the highest point on the Mall in Mussoorie.

The large open flat near St Paul's Church has a small park, flanked by the famous 'Char Dukan', literally meaning four shops: Bipin's Tiptop Teashop, Anil's Coffee Joint, a Bank, and Surbir's Cyber Cafe. 'Eggetarians' (vegetarians who eat eggs) can go to Bipin's or Anil's to

LEFT: The exterior of St Paul's Church at Char Dukan.

ABOVE: St Paul's Church in the Cantonment was consecrated on 1st May 1840 to fulfill the spiritual needs of the British troops quartered at the Landour's Convalescent Depot. It has just been restored to its original glory.

have a fill of cheese-fillet omelettes with buns or try out some of the savoury french fries. They are crisp, fresh, and highly recommended.

It was just the other day, I saw this rather plump visiting professor on a lecture tour at the Landour Language School. With more chins than a Delhi Telephone Directory, he was tucking into his fourth plate of cheese toasts, muttering to the boy serving his table: 'I miss my wife's cooking—as often as I can.'

Actor Victor Banerjee's home in Landour, at the Parsonage, has a board outside his home that warns trespassers: 'Beware Rabid Thespian'. Do not get intimidated by this. He is the most genial of hosts and if you go see him by appointment, you will meet the quintessential Bengali Bhadralok, literally meaning 'a well-

mannered person'. When I last saw our very own thespian, better known for his offbeat roles in films like *Home in the World*, *Bitter Moon* and *A Passage to India*, he was fortified by an aromatic brew of King Nettle, and was off to the remote interiors of Uttarakhand, in pursuit of the elusive Yeti!

If you get the eerie feeling that, the mural on the rock-face at his gate is staring at you, it is! Pele, the Mother Goddess of volcanoes, from Hawaii, misses little. So does our actor! Author Ruskin Bond, Landour's blue-eyed boy, is not far behind in that sense. From atop his eyrie at Ivy Cottage, he watches the goings-on in the Mohalla down below.

For 40 years now, I have watched him ferreting rare recipes and, he is tight, especially with these, behaving like a Himalayan magpie in collecting all sorts of perfectly useless beads and baubles and facts. Just the other day, he claimed to have perfected a secret recipe to boil an egg but refuses to part with it because the eggs might look like clones! Hopefully, one of these days you will come across Ruskin Bond's bestseller entitled: 'Hundred Ways of How to Boil an Egg'.

Most of the older residents of Landour have long departed, but their old houses are still in use. Their present owners, the famous and the wealthy, live elsewhere and visit the place once in a while. It is everyone's dream to own a house in Landour but once a property has been bought and done up nicely, it is usually forgotten. A majority of the Landour Cantonment houses lie empty for most of the year. Luckily, there are some residents like Prannoy and Radhika Roy of New Delhi Television, who succumb to the song of the sirens of Landour and return again and again to their home Bellevue—perched above the mouth of Sister Bazaar.

But I have digressed... If you take a left from Char Dukan, crossing a sturdy bridge, you are at the commencement of the Landour Mall, or western Circular Road, a very pleasant road, running northward under Wolfsburn, past Shamrock to the entrance of St Asaphs. Then

FACING PAGE TOP: At Church Flat, today's Char Dukan, one saw immaculately whitewashed houses with red roofs of those early days which were in harmony with a pleasure resort like Mussoorie. In the hills, you just could not build anywhere. Trees, lawns and extensive grounds provided the right atmosphere of tranquility.

FACING PAGE BELOW LEFT: Actor Victor Banerjee lauded for his roles in films like Satyajit Ray's 'Home in the World' and David Lean's 'A Passage to India', came for a film-shoot to Landour in 1982, fell in love with the place and has made Landour his home.

FACING PAGE BELOW RIGHT: A sign outside the Parsonage. Victor and Maya spend as much time as they possibly can in their quaint cottage.

it turns back along the northeast face of the hill, between the two cemeteries: the Protestant and the Catholic, under the Language School to the Ellangowan junction, from where it goes back to the Church under Rokeby.

Folk up here in Landour tend to look down on Mussoorie. They think of it as a raffish place of traffic jams that is trying hard not to look like Delhi's crowded Chandni Chowk or Ajmal Khan Road on a busy day. And why not? Landour's two Upper Malls are real promenades where you can take a walk under a canopy of oak and deodar trees and hear the cicadas strike up their shrill sword-on-grindstone symphony.

Remember when you are 7,000 ft high in the sky, enveloped by the ambrosial air of the Himalayas, in God's own land, with cakes and ale, there is not much else one can ask for. Just the other day, a note was found dropped by some visitor in actor Victor Banerjee's letter box which aptly illustrates the feeling:

'We are yet another tourist couple from the plains who could not take their eyes off your house. Needless to say, it is by far the most beautiful house we have ever seen. Staring at it quite shamelessly despite your presence was in some way beyond our control. If you noticed two detectives look-alike with characteristic long black overcoats and dark glasses, we apologise profusely for the intrusion on your privacy. Although, we must admit that fighting the temptation to knock on your door (notwithstanding the loyal presence of your pet) was rather difficult.

For every random stroller in this beautiful place who is looking for nothing but a peaceful moment or two, your home only adds to the serenity.

May you continue to lend inspiring moments to more tourists and wanderers like us.'

The symphony of cicadas reaches a crescendo in the monsoon.

A walk down the narrow lanes of Landour where the buildings lean against each other as if for comfort.

And so, Landour remains like an island of calm in a sea of troubles, where you can still hear the wind whispering in the deodars.

Today, in the bazaar, you will still find small shops leaning against each other as if for comfort. Stop at any little store: the chemist, the draper, the tailor or the watch-repairer and you will find that in almost every family, a child who has studied in one of the schools here, has gone for advanced education overseas. They have made it to Harvard, Cambridge, and MIT. You name it and they have done it. In our little town, the accessibility to higher education have opened new doors for the next generation and has brought about a change that no economic miracle could have ever achieved. Could there be a better way of building tomorrow?

What else remains the same in Mussoorie and Landour?

Two things spring to mind: the view of the Garhwal Himalaya (indeed, the very same view of Banderpoonch that Hyder Jung Hearsey saw nearly 200 years ago!) from the bend on the Upper Mall near Lal Tibba and then, in autumn, seen from Balahissar, on the old Kipling Road above Barlowganj, the magnificent displays of sheets and forks lightning in the valley down below.

Table of Distances

From	To	Distance (Approx)
LBSNAA Gate	Company Bagh	2 Km
	The Park	4 Km
	Benog	9 Km
	Kempty Falls	6 Km Via Chakrata Road
	Evelyn Hall	3 Km
	Kulri	4 Km
	Picture Palace	4 Km
The Library	Company Bagh	4 Km Via Charleville Gate
	The Park	4 Km Via The Convent
	Benog	9 Km Via The Convent
	Kempty Falls	8 Km Via Chakrata Road
	Cottage Hospital	1.2 Km Via The Gorge
	Kulri	2 Km
	Picture Palace	2 Km
	Landour Bazaar	3 Km
	Barlowganj	5 Km
	Mossy Falls	7 Km
	Kincraig	2 Km Via Cart Road
	Jharipani	8 Km Via Cart Road
	Rajpur	14 Km Via Old Cart Road
Picture Palace	Cottage Hospital	1 Km
	Company Bagh	4 Km
	The Park	6 Km
	Kempty Falls	10 Km
	Landour Bazaar	1 Km
	Barlowganj	3 Km
	Mossy Falls	4 Km
	Oak Grove School	7 Km
General Post Office	Barlowganj	3 Km
	Half-Way House	7 Km
	Rajpur	13 Km
	Sahastradhara Springs	18 Km Via Bridle Path
	Dehradun Railway Station	24 Km

CIRCUITS: Round Camel's Back, including the Mall 4 km Sunny View to Dehra Railway Station 34 km (Motor Road)

From	To	Distance (Approx)
Clock Tower	All Saint's Church	1 Km
	Benog Observatory	12 Km Via Library
	Barlowganj	2 Km
	Bhatta Falls	4 Km Via Sebastopol, Barlowganj Onto Bhatta
	Christ Church	2 Km
	Happy Valley	5 Km
	St Mary's Hospital	2 Km
	Jharipani	4 Km Via Sebastopol, Old Rajpur Road
	Kempty Falls	10 Km Via Library, Happy Valley, Polo Ground
	Mossy Falls	2 Km Via Sebastopol
	Company Bagh	4 Km
	Murray Falls	6 Km Via Dhobi Ghat
	Mussoorie Library	3 Km
	Old Race Course/Polo Ground	6 Km Via Library
	Priest Garden	3 Km Khatapani
	Rajpur	10 Km Via Old Bridle Path
	St Paul's Church, Landour	2 Km
Library, Mussoorie	Benog Observatory	10 Km
	Barlowganj	5 Km Via Mackinnon Cart Road
	Bhatta Falls	6 Km Past Bhatta Village
	Christ Church	½ Km
	Happy Valley	2 Km
	Jharipani	2 Km
	Kempty Fall	10 Km Via Happy Valley, Polo Ground
	Mossey Falls	5 Km Via Lodge Dalhousie
	Company Bagh	2 Km
	Murray Falls	11 Km
	Priest Garden	5 Km Khatapani
	St Paul's Church, Landour	4 Km
St Paul's Church, Landour Cantonment	Benog Observatory	14 Km
	Barlowganj	4 Km
	Bhatta Falls	9 Km
	Christ Church	6 Km
	Happy Valley	7 Km
	St Mary's Hospital	6 Km
	Jharipani	7 Km
	Kempty Falls	12 Km
	Kulri	3 Km
	Mossey Falls	6 Km
	Company Bagh	6 Km
	Mussoorie Library	4 Km
	Rajpur	14 Km

CIRCUITS: Three hills of Landour Cantonment 5 km Waverley Circuit 4 km

Section Two

From the Archives

The first guide to Mussoorie was written
when the place was just over 50 years old

Guide to

Masuri, Landaur, Dehradun

&

The Hills North of Dehra

By

John Northam

Editor & Proprietor,
'Himalaya Chronicle', Masuri
Printed: Calcutta: Thacker, Spink & Co. 1884

'Extract from reprint (2006)
kind courtesy Hugh Rayner, Pagoda Tree Press U.K.'

1

Description of the Country

HENCESOVER the traveller may hail, it will be convenient to consider him asleep from the time he puts his foot into the railway carriage until the glare and bustle of the Saháranpur platform arouses him to the contemplation of a long and tedious journey in a dâk gharry.

It forms no part of the writer's present purpose to descant upon the inconveniences of overcrowded railway carriages—a matter which will form the topic for the newspapers during the beginning and latter end of the hill season. We may say, however, that happy is the traveller who, by exercise of a little foresight, comes early to the railway station, and secures his comfortable seat, while the tardy passenger is a mile away from the station vociferously urging on the ghariwan to an impracticable speed – a vain performance, which is usually followed by the penalty of having to sit and sleep on his own boxes, after bestowing a few anathemas on the railway authorities in general and their rolling-stock in particular. There never was a place like an Indian terminal railway station, in the month of April, to illustrate the immense advantage of being in time. Be instructed then, gentle reader and be in time. But what shall we say of the wretched traveller who may be kicking his heels on the broad promenade of an intermediate station, or the unhappy half-dozen passengers which a branch train has disgorged for transmission into the approaching mail. Being in time has no advantages for them. The scriptural camel passing through the eye of a needle was no greater puzzle than the question as to where the traveller and the multitude of his belongings are to be stowed away. But we have too many troubles of our own to permit more than a passing sympathy, and must needs leave every hapless creature to bear his own burdens, while we hurry on to Saháranpur.

Still we may pause awhile to point out how many kinds of travellers there are who move hillwards during the hot and rainy seasons.

First, there are those who never fail to go every season as regularly and punctually as clock-work. They are in great part matronly ladies surrounded by a graded assortment of young olive branches who could not live in the plains, you know, in the hot weather. The olive branches develop into ruddy little cherubs in the balmy air of Masúri for the orthodox ten days "sky," making it fourteen by dodging in the Saturdays and Sundays.

There is another kind of lady who migrates to the hills with punctuality of the swallow's flight. Nature has not been bountiful to her in the way of olive branches, and, with not particular ties, she leaves her husband in the plains. She is lonesome and disconsolate, of course; may be she does not take long to correct her loneliness, and a strong effort may dissipate the sadness of her depressing situation; for why should she drag on her weary footsteps through six months, "the world forgetting, by the world forgot." In some instances, only a few, of course, within a little month – nay, not so much, not one – she is one of the most impassioned devotees of the Masúri slide,

and, perchance, may have a "bow-wow," a harmless creature who, for the sake of her innocent company, is willing to fetch and carry, and dance a regular attendance. The most discerning know that all this does not travel beyond the paths of rectitude, although censorious people will nod their heads over it. It has passed into a custom, and although probably more "honoured in the breach than the observance," the fact that it is a custom – or the fashion – takes much of the sting out of the censure of Mrs. Grundy.

Besides those in active service, there are a larger number of retired military men in Masúri and Lándaur than in any other hill-station. Colonels, Majors-General, Lieutenants-General, their familiar faces are well known. They are quite harmless and kind-hearted, and being good-humoured jolly fellows, they become deservedly popular. In the cold weather they are to be found at Dehra, Mirath, or Agra, and many other places, and sometimes stay up in the hills great-coated and muffled up to the chin. The migratory retired officer fixes his journey to Masúri with the precision of the almanac.

Then there is the advent of the mercantile community, the ladies and gentlemen who open establishments for the disposal of various articles of merchandize, all of exceeding good quality, but too numerous to mention. They come up early and fix a day for opening out, long antecedent to the arrival of their stock. This gives a little for recreation, which usually takes the form of hurling maledictions, loud and deep, at the devote heads of Messrs. Buckle & Co., the carrying agents, whose rolling-stock, like that of the railway companies, is excusably insufficient for a glut of traffic. The head of that enterprising film has hitherto survived the severest forms of anathema, and the writer is credibly informed he still lives.

The young subaltern, who takes his sixty days' *con amore*, must not be forgotten. Some plunge at once into the vortex of a two months' pleasure, at the beginning of the season, before it has been well aired, and manage, lucky dogs, to run up for another two months at the close. There are two kinds of subalterns – one the amorous, the other the jolly. The former usually fall into lines of bow-wow-ism. Of course, they are members or invitees of the Club, they reunionise, get up balls and dances, and nice little picnics, besides buying *nic-nacs*, which some people have the audacity to say they find difficulty in paying for; the other representative of the subaltern is he who is a good-natured and rollicking specimen of a Queen's officer, and who has not been weak enough to have his locks shorn by Delilah. He plays billiards and smokes cheroots the most of his time, and, with rare exception, knows when he has had safe number of pegs. The recent wars in Afghanistan and Egypt have chevied the subaltern about a good deal, and, for the last few season and in the height of Masúri enjoyment, he has been called down suddenly to join his regiment, and curtailed the number of Masúri society.

But who is that place and wan-looking lady, or that yellow-skinned gentleman, being taken up hill in a jampan? Their pinched countenances wear the evidence of inward pain; anybody can tell why they are going up to Masúri. They go to seek what they may not find. If the change does not cure them, they increase the length of a certain register in the keeping of the Chaplain of Masúri, and occupy a final resting-place beneath the beautiful flowers in the local cemetery. This must happen to some of course, but there are more who pick up their strength, and go down comparatively hale and hearty. Yes, it is a great *omnium gatherum* that, during the season, fills to overflowing the popular sanitarium of Masúri, about which we shall have much more to say by-and-by.

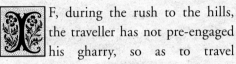

2

From Saharanpur

IF, during the rush to the hills, the traveller has not pre-engaged his gharry, so as to travel northwards during the night, he has little chance of starting until the next morning, and the impatient excursionist has the mortification of seeing gharry after gharry depart hillwards to the lively though unmusical sound of the coachman's bugle. It is an ill-wind that blows nobody good, and one of the several hotels, or the dâk bungalow, will profit by the wayfarer's discomfiture. If nobody takes precedence of him, he may be sent on at midnight, which is the commencement of the dâk gharry day.

If he be fortunate enough to find a disengaged gharry, by starting about 8 or 9 P.M., he has every chance of getting into Rájpur by about 5 or 6 in the morning; but it would be as well not to lay wagers about this matter, because dâk gharries are frequently found to be indifferently constituted vehicles, and the tats self-willed and unreliable. Starting at midnight the *masáfar* might reach Rájpur in time for breakfast, and get up to Masúri in the middle of the day. But this is rather fore-stalling matters.

At the time of the hillward flight, there is no practical purpose to be attained by haggling with any of the dâk chaprassies: they will not be beaten down, they will have their pound of flesh. One would think with so much competition a modification of full fares might be bargained for, but the *munshi* is deaf to any persuasion that proposes to curtail his fares. But this rigid exaction of full fares is partly due to an organisation called an "amalgamation" – an institution through which all the dâk gharry proprietors combine to charge nothing less than full fares, and run in turns, so that the traffic is pretty equally divided. The full dák gharry rates from Saharánpur to Rájpur are as follows:-

	Rs
One full gharry (two inside and one out)	40
Two outside and one in	35
One in and one out	30
One inside seat only	25
The mail-cart seat costs	11

Besides this it is advisable to tip the coachman, if he behaves well.

If the traveller's business, or pleasure, is not very urgent, he will be a gainer by a delay until the morning, for by pushing on overnight, he loses the sight of much that is worthy of a passing view, notably the Siwálik range of hills, which, with the further off Himalayas, closes in the lovely valley of the Dehra Dún. The dák *chaukis*, or stages, from Saharánpur to Rájpur, at the foot of the Masúri hills, are as follows:-

Miles.

Kailaspur	
Harorá	
Chatmalpur	14
Naddi	
Guneshpur	
Mohan	28
Túnbárá	⎫
Landibara	⎬ in the Mohan pass
Asaruri	36

Bhim Tal	
Dehra	42
Bodyguard Lines	
Rájpur	49

The reader will not find much to interest him until his arrival at Mohan. The road is generally in good order, especially up to Fathipur, a short distance on the north side of Chatmalpur. The tats are pretty good goers for the first stage, but after that it is one long struggle between man and beast.

The vice of a large proportion of the horses on the line consists in a most pronounced objection to start. The virtuous *tats* are decidedly in the minority. The *tat* at length comes to the conclusion that he had better do his stage and be done with it; and off he bounds at full gallop, in which he is encouraged by the coachman, who knows very well that the slightest check would entail another quarter hour of hard swearing and hard work.

Then the long waits at the *chaukis* are most tantalizing, especially at night. The sound of the bugle conveys no warning to a sleeping *bálgir*, but by dint of loud shouting a far off ventriloquial sound is heard like the muffled voice of the man in the coal-cellar, and after a leisurely contemplation of all the circumstances and surroundings of the position, the *bálgir* drags the unwilling *tats* forth. The coachman retires for his forty whiffs from the hubble-bubble, and then recommences the old coaxing and maledictions, until we again roll on our way. Happy is the man who at night can sleep through all this, until the rising sun shows him the Masúri hills straight in front, with its white houses glowing in the early morning light.

But if the traveller is not in so very great a hurry to reach the hills, he will find a day journey much more agreeable, and a flying visit to the Saháranpur gardens, as well as to the stables of the Remount Department, both highly interesting. There is very little to entertain one on the road up to Mohan, except to count the small furlong pillarettes, until they get to the big milestone, which tells you how far you are from Saháranpur, and how many more of them you have to pass before you get to Dehra. From Mohan these milestones first open their minds about the distance to Rájpur.

At Chatmalpur, just short of Fathipur, the wild road and open ground looks cheery, and here the highway to Rúrki branches off both from Saháranpur and Masúri. Near this spot stands a dák bungalow, wherein an hour and-a-half's patience will probably secure you a spatch cock presumedly hatched during the Mutiny. At Naddi and Guneshpur the same order of things prevails. But at Mohan, the stage which lies at the southern extremity of the Siwálik range, the scene is a very pleasing one with the river on the right, as well as one of the prettiest and most ample encamping-grounds in India. Mohan rejoices in a post office, vernacular schools, and a dák bungalow, perched upon a picturesque knoll, commands a view of much of the Saháranpur District, with little peeps of wooded hill scenery. Sportsmen generally take to canvas, and are, therefore, independent of dák bungalows. The bungalow, though, is very popular, and supplies, beyond the ubiquitous chicken, can be had on due notice being given. Honeymoons have been frequently initiated there, and the contemplation of that well-known fact leads one to consider that no time should be lost in giving some account of the Siwáliks to which Mohan forms the southern gate.

3

Onward

E will proceed on our journey through the pass, commencing at the twenty-first milestone from Rájpur, at the foot of the hills. The first part of the pass has a very gentle gradient, that of the latter part being more severe and winding. The scenery is very pretty, every turn of the road bringing a fresh view to the eye. A trip through the Mohan pass by daylight, specially to those unaccustomed to mountain scenery, is a real enjoyment which can only be adequately attested by experience. The succession of peaks sloping one above the other, the more prominent crests clad with sal or the pine to the north-east, and on the south-west presenting a bare perpendicular precipice as straightly cut as the wall of a huge fort, kept bare and clean by the drenching fury of the south-west monsoons. The *tats* usually go at a swingeing pace up to and across the girder bridge and on to Túnbárá, a *chauki* nesting on the right under a high rock covered with thick jungle, on the left being the river bed, backed by those irrepressible peaks so wild and weird in their appearance. At Landibárá, the next stage, the gradient becomes severe, and some of the dák companies treat the traveller with bullocks instead of horses, up to the tunnel and on to Asaruri. Two miles an hour for a bullock is almost a dangerously swift pace, and, in order not to shock the nerves of delicate passengers, he occasionally considerately reduces it to one, with occasional intervals of rest, about which latter the bullocks and the drivers frequently entertain a serious difference of opinion. Landibárá is a capital place to get out and stretch one's legs. Any ordinary pedestrian will find it a very pleasant walk from Landibárá to the tunnel. Saunter along as slowly as he possibly can, he is safe to reach the tunnel about three-quarters of an hour before the bullocks.

But the blessed law of compensation comes in here, as in almost everything, and the solace of the pipe, or even two, may reconcile him to the petty annoyances of the world in general, and the dilatoriness of dák bullocks in particular. He even sympathizes with the poor creatures, as he hears down in the deep distance below the thwack of the driver's cudgel, as it comes into violent contact with the poor animal's hide. To impart an agreeable finish to this performance, the driver screams and yells in a tongue unknown, except to those whose profession is to urge on unwilling animals of locomotion, and are adepts in the art of tail-twisting. The short tunnel, pierced through the crown of that part of the range, relieves the traveller of a severer ascent experienced by the traveller of former days. The excellent road, too, cut through the pass parallel to the bed of the Mohan, gives us an immense advantage over former travellers who had to invoke the aid of the *dúli-wállas*, who took their freight up the bed of the river, so frequently impassable, however, on account of the constantly recurrent downpours of the rainy season. The bridges and culverts along the road are so numerous that one gets as tired of noting them as one does in counting off the furlong stones across the plain from Saháranpur.

In the days of the *dúli*, travelling through the Mohan pass was not so invulnerable as it is now. Wild beasts were occasionally troublesome, and frequently insisted on scraping an acquaintance with the wayfarer. The wild elephant, which even now abounds in the Siwáliks, often rendered himself inconveniently familiar. After gratifying his curiosity in respect to the personal appearance and general surroundings of the traveller, he might walk off harmlessly in an opposite direction, for the elephant, being a pure vegetarian, obtains no personal advantage by an attack on a human being as an article of diet. But there is a tide in the affairs of male elephants, which taken at the flood leads on to danger to the traveller, and at the slightest provocation the elephant lashes himself into an ungovernable fury, when woe-betide all living creatures that cross his path. The elephant has still a "local habitation" in the Siwáliks, "and a name" for being subject to this degrading influence. There have been occasions when travellers have given up a night journey, in consequence of a report that a *must* elephant is paying a visit to the highways and by-ways of civilization, as represented by the road through the Mohan pass. An elephant, in this deplorable condition, is a dangerous customer to meet on the road, for although he reaps no advantage by committing "culpable homicide amounting to murder," he, under the influence of temporary insanity, is seized with an ungovernable desire to crouch up a *ghari* like a matchbox, and trample the traveller into a jelly. But the reader must not be frightened, for it is long since any accident occurred from the attacks of wild animals, which invariably avoid the haunts of man and live a life of close retirement. In the old *dúli* days, flaring torches and abundant tom-tom-ing were generally successful in protecting the traveller.

Well, to proceed on our journey. On going down a hill, the bullock, as well as the ghari pony, shows off his paces to the best advantage; the couple of miles or so to Asarúri, a village on the western bank of the *rao* of that name, is got over quickly. We are here on the skirts of a forest where game abounds, and where the wild boar has his lair. If the traveller has come through the pass by night, he might, in the very early dawn (he will still be 13 miles from the foot of the hills,) yearn for a cup of tea, which luxury can be supplied him from a tumble-down "shanty" on a hillock above the road, and which people, in generous moments, have called a "rest-house." The traveller may even indulge in the extravagance of boiled eggs and bread and butter. The style of architecture of the "shanty" is lost in the chronic state of its disrepair. There are rooms, but they are in an advanced state of ventilation, the furniture being practically *nil*, because nobody risks his life by going inside. A man or woman of great courage might sit on the verandah if one of the two chairs does not collapse under his or her weight, and a thump on the rickety teapoy would reduce it to fragments. Honeymoons have been kept there, too; but that was long ago. On a consideration of all the circumstances and probabilities of the case, the traveller usually acts upon the conclusion that the safer place to partake of refreshment is in his *ghari.*

So, on we go Dehra-wards, stopping at a penal settlement - looking kind of a place called Bhimtal, where we again change horses. All along the gentle slope, through the forest land, from Asarúri, we have the glorious sight of the *lower* Himalayas straight in front, with the white buildings of Masúri and Lándaur crowning the highest visible points, or nestling on the southern slopes of the Masúri amphitheatre. Before reaching Dehra, we cross the Bindal *naddi* – a performance easy enough except in the rains, when it forms a mountain torrent, which is frequently unfordable. Travellers have been known to be kept, waiting on the wrong side of the stream for seven hours, wearily watching for the ebb of the torrent – a calamity, however, which happens only during the rainy season. We pass through the native street, or bazaar, of Dehra, where we again change horses, and proceed through the best part of the European quarter. But we must hurry on to Masúri and leave all notice of Dehra and the lovely Dún for a future chapter. Near the viceroy's Body-guard lines, the hot weather quarters of those fine fellows who are charged with the safety of the Viceregal person, another and last change is made about three miles from Rájpur. From the Bodyguard lines to Rájpur the traveller is indulged with three, and frequently four, *tats*. The explanation of this is found in the fact that Rájpur is 600 and odd feet above the level of Dehra, and therefore this last stage of the journey requires greater horse-power.

The coachman, happy in having come to the end of his journey, blows his bugle more cheerily as he enters the pretty little plateau at the foot of the Rájpur bazar. Mentioning the coachman's bugle, a keyless instrument like the old post-horns in England of days gone by, the traveller, before he arrives at Rájpur, will have learnt the uses of this instrument. It is sounded to clear the road of those obstinate country carts and other obstructions, as also to warn the establishment at the approaching stage that horses are wanted. The writer, after considerable experience, does not believe it expedites, in the slightest degree, the movements of the *saises* in charge, but the coachman blows his bugle in the simple indulgence of a pleasant fiction. The name of a coachman is generally known by his cadences, which are entirely original, he being his own composer, and occasionally indulging in *impromptu* variations of the most whimsical character, and utterly independent of all musical conventionalities. On entering Rájpur he shows great form and the bugle has rather a hard time of it. These dulcet strains put the hotel-keepers on the qui vive, for one of the five places of entertainment will profit by the new arrival and four will be disappointed as the *ghari* rolls into another compound. As to the bugle, two or three of the coachmen, out of the whole, approach "within measurable distance" of art. The plateau before-mentioned is one great hostelry for the entertainment of man and beast. There are the Ellenborough, the Rájpur, and the Prince of Wales, as well as "Agency Retiring-rooms" and a Resthouse, the latter under native superintendence. How they all manage to exist is a puzzle; but they keep the shutters down year after year, and presumably live on their losses. They all furnish fair entertainment, and administer to one's comforts with commendable solicitude and at very moderate rates. Having made his choice of a hotel, probably the first matter that strikes the traveller's attention is the necessity for a good tub, which can be had, hot or cold, on the shortest notice.

4

Roads to Masuri

AVING breakfasted, or taken tiffin, as the case may be, it is desirable for the traveller to see his luggage weighed and dispatched, so as to give the coolies a good start, for these sturdy fellows take at least four hours to reach the heart of Masúri, and longer if his destination be Western Masúri, and along towards the Happy Valley. In any case, the traveller invariably overtakes his personal belongings on the road upwards. If his journey to Rájpur should end in the evening, he will dine and sleep at one of the hotels, for the bridle-path up to Masúri is rather hazardous to a stranger on horseback, although the night-ride is commonly accomplished by residents familiar with the road. The coolies, except under enormous pressure and abundant *backshish*, will never take one up in a dandy or jampan after dark. The hill man and the fairer and more sturdy *pachmis*, who hail from the neighbourhood of the Kangra Valley, are superstitious, and believe in hobgoblins of sorts; moreover he has a wholesome dread of wild beasts, and experience not infrequently justifies his fears. Recently a man was frightfully mauled by a bear on one of the roads up to Masúri. There are only two modes of locomotion up the hill to Masúri - that is riding on horseback or being carried. A good livery horse can be got from most of the hotels for Rs. 2-8, and a bazaar *tat* for much less, occasionally so low as As. 12. Any gentleman not accustomed to the saddle had better eschew the assistance of a quadruped, for, for the most part, the road is steep, and in the early part of the journey exceedingly so; so that an untrained rider, unaccustomed to equestrianism on the hills, in all probability, "will not remain," but slither over the animal's tail; certainly to keep possession of the saddle he will be compelled, in many parts, to hold on with great tenacity to the many or the pummel – an operation by no means graceful or becoming. One accustomed to the saddle will get on well enough. Those whose equestrian education has been neglected had better be carried up in a jampan or a dandy. A jampan, it is presumed, may come under the generic term of a vehicle, although it does not run on wheels; but it is, at all events, an instrument of locomotion which should be seen to be understood. Its body somewhat resembles an easy chair, at the corners of which are horizontal poles, which support the roof covered with oil-cloth to keep out the rain. Ring curtains are fixed in such a way that the occupant can slide them so that the curtains may intercept the hot rays of the sun, or protect him from dirty weather. The motive-power consists of eight coolies, four at a time, who take their places between the projecting horizontal poles in front and rear. At either end a leather strap connects the two poles, through which a shoulder stick runs; one *cooly* takes one part of the stick on his shoulder, the other, and it is in this way the hill visitor is shaken, tossed, and jolted for the weary seven miles to Masúri. A dandy is a much more comprehendable conveyance than a jampan, and is solely dedicated to the light weights. It is a canoe-shaped arrangement, the bottom, in which the traveller sits, with his legs in a horizontal position, is made generally out of *darri*, the frame being oval in form with a projection of each end for the cooly's shoulder. Eight men are the usual complement for a jampan, four for a dandy. A jampan and the coolies will cost Rs. 3 or Rs. 3-8; a dandy about Rs. 2 all included.

The tourist or visitor having seen that everything is ready, mounts his pony, or scrambles into his jampan or dandy, and starts for Masúri. There is nearly a mile of sloping bazar to get through before he gets into the open road, with his nose close to the hills, which tower one above the other, laden with vegetation. On the right, down in the deep Khud, below, runs the *Raspanna naddi*, emerging from the hills northwards, and threading the narrow entrance to the Dehra Dún, the stream being diverted into the canal, which, after being augmented by the watershed contributed by innumerable streams and riverlets, runs through and fertilizes nearly the whole of the Western Dún. The sigh of the water of the *naddi* as it washes the boulders where it emerges into the cultivated valley, and its roar when the rainfall converts it into a seething torrent, are pleasant to listen to from the height above. A little out of Rájpur, there is a toll-bar, where each laden cooly has to pay a pice; the toll for a jampan being eight annas; a dandy, four annas; a horse, four annas; and a pony (under 13 hands), two annas. A few years ago, only half these rates were demanded, but Masúri is improving rapidly, and money was wanted, whereupon the then Lieutenant-Governor sanctioned the increase of the tolls for the privilege of entering the gate of paradise as represented by a cool and bracing climate. From the toll-gate there are two roads to Masúri, - one straight up the steepest and the most frequented route, seven miles in distance, the precipitous acclivities being surmounted by the ingenious zig-zag road cut into the mountain side. The other road bears to the left from the toll-bar, and the length of which is variously estimated to cover from ten to fourteen miles of ground to the library; and as the gradient is light compared to the other road, and although it winds round the hills in long sweeps, it is not marked by those zig-zag turns and twists which characterize the shorter cut. This road is called Mackinnon's road, after the name of the designer and constructor, supported by a combination of capital contributed by those who had an interest in securing wheeled traffic to and from Masúri. It was for a long time practicable for country carts, but heavy rains caused landslips, especially where the treacherous *kállá matti*, or black earth, obtruded itself, and which from its extreme friability was constantly giving way and completely blocking up the road. It was abandoned or a long time and became completely impassable. With the advent of Messrs. Whymper & Co., however, who leased the Crown Brewery in 1876, the road was again repaired by them and carts constructed for carrying beer in wood, and fitted with breaks, which are frequently found necessary in steadying the pace down-hill. This road is extremely picturesque, having the advantage of a good view of the Dún and Siwáliks most of the way. It is rather a dull journey on horseback without company, although, in consequence of the comparatively easy gradient, with a good horse or pony, the rider may go at a trot or a light canter all the way. This pleasant road, however, is mainly dedicated to the transmission of John Barleycorn; to the fair hill maiden, who having herded her cattle, which have browsed in the adjacent jungles, drives them to the near village; and to the light hearted *pahári* swain, who tootles on his rude wooden pipe as he returns, with a gay heart and a light step, from his daily labour. Matters in this direction are eminently pastoral, the important village of Bhatta being passed through as we near Masúri. The *pahári* villages round about are noted for their pretty hill girls, and on festive occasions, when the toilet has added its charms to their persons, some of these hill lasses are really handsome. At weddings they show off to the best advantage, as it is befitting they should, as they flock in thousands, decked in all the colours of the rainbow, to the festive scene.

The more direct road presents a very different sight, as your pony toils up the zig-zag highway, or as the jámpánis cant you most uncomfortably up and down with their swingeing stride. Here the road is full of traffic of all sorts. The tats, mules, and donkeys, broken kneed and cow hocked, are slithering down the hill on their return journey, unladen, having left Rájpur that morning with their heavy burdens, containing supplies for Masúri and Lándaur, before there was the slightest sign of the approaching morn. They are far up the hill by the time the grey, which heralds the flush of the approaching sunrise, tips the eastern hills, and when they get to Rájpur or Dehra again, their day's work is done. As you go slowly along, you overtake battalions of coolies, with burdens on their heads, and huge trunks and boxes, bedding, and the multitudinous varieties of personal belongings, are fastened to men's backs, the panting coolies, every now and then, taking advantage of some friendly shelf or protuberance in the rock to take a brief rest. Then there may be seen the coolies from the forwarding agencies with the more ponderous *aswab*, which has come by luggage train to Saháranpur, and sent on by bullock cart to Rájpur. The names and addresses on these boxes and packages, large and small, from a brandy box to a grand piano, form almost a complete directory of Masúri and Lándaur. It takes only one man to carry a case of wine or spirits, and there *is* a precious lot of it going up, but for a piano or a bale of merchandize, it may take from 16 to 20 men. There is scarcely any break in this stream of traffic. Then there are the more domestic features of the scene. At the period of migration into Masúri or Lándaur, the native general dealers, the sugar boilers, the bakers, the butchers the crockery-men, toy-makers, lohi-walas, *cum multis aliis*, transmigrate their domesticities, and astride a miserable hill-tat, may be seen the *guid* wife, with an olive branch, sometimes two, perched upon its withers. Paterfamilias keeps alongside as best he can on Shanks' pony, as he hears the clank, clank, of his cooking utensils in charge of the cooly struggling behind. Then along may come the stupid-looking little *dúli* of a *pardanashin*, who takes little peeps, herself unseen at her surroundings. The perspiring husband keeps alongside with anxious mien, and prenez garde is his motto. Then there are *kitmatgárs* and *bearers*, many of them bearing their own burdens, *saises* leading the horses of their *sahibs*, who are coming tomorrow or next day, or have gone ahead that morning. Then there are sweepers with dogs of various breeds, or no breed at all, the poor creatures being nearly dead with thirst and fatigue. Besides these there are the poorer and sicklier lot of men and women, and nobody seems to know why they are going to Masúri. The man has, we will say, *per example* literally taken up his bed and walked. Fixed upon the *chárpai* are most of his goods and chattels, consisting of a few cooking utensils, and a dirty and ragged-looking *resai* or two, with the ever present hubble-bubble. The woman in the agony of blistered feet, and panting under the distress of physical exhaustion, carries a child, innocent of clothing, across her lean and angular hips, and misery sits on the countenances of all of them. Sometimes a flock of sheep or geese may be panting on the journey up-hill. Some of them give up from exhaustion, and frequently have to be carried. These eventually find their way to the dinner tables of Masúri and Lándaur at the time of the rush up. There is very little traffic met going down-hill from Masúri and Lándaur, except the returning *tats*, mules, and donkeys, who nearly smother one with the terrible dust they kick up. In October and November, the order of traffic is reversed. Then there is a general stampede from the hills, as though Masúri and Lándaur were afflicted with the plague. Leaves are then expiring and visitors are resuming their cold weather routine in the plains, the ladies, especially, lingering on long into November. March, October and November are the most enjoyable months in the year on the hills.

There is little else to attract the traveller, but the stream of traffic, though occasional peeps over the lovely valley below, attract the eye from the incidents of the road. This road to Masúri has suffered more abuse than any other highway in India, and the writer regrets that he is not in a position to accept a brief for the defence. At some places, it is cut into solid rock, at others into a loose shale or slate-stone formation, with here and there bits of black earth through which no road can be maintained. The natural and uncivilized state of this road if left alone would be, that where hard limestone formed its base, there would a lilliputian rocky range of small hillocks and mountainettes jutting up and rendering the roads, either on horse or foot, immensely trying to man or beast. Where the shale or slate-stones abound, the road is covered with snagged-shaped *debris* fallen from above; while the black earth, more sand than gravel, embraces a horse's hoof a foot deep. The mode adopted for repairing or making the road passable is to throw loose earth on its face – a system of levelling up. Where the slate-stones are, loose earth is thrown down in the vain hope of its binding the pointed snags; the black earth is incorrigible and must be endured. Immediately after this top-dressing, the road forms excellent going; but the hot season bakes it into powder, and the hoofs of horses and the feet of men triturate it into a dust, which rises up into clouds on being disturbed. Or, again, the fury of a heavy shower of the steady downpour of the first rains wash the whole *debris* down the *khuds*, and the road reassumes its rough and rugged character to the discomfort of all concerned in it proper repair. Surely the engineering skill of India can supply a better means of keeping a hill road in repair than that of throwing down the *debris* of the banks, to level down the protuberances, hillocks, or mountainettes, which *debris* may be blown up by the wind or washed by the rain on the first opportunity. Unfortunately or fortunately, some say fortunately, Masúri has no gubernatorial visitors, otherwise an attack of gravel rash sustained by a real Lieutenant-Governor might be the preliminary of successful repairs, or the construction of a new road which has been talked about for years without being commenced. The road is much too steep for comfortable travelling, and a new one with easier gradients and practicable bases is a decided want of Masúri and Lándaur.

Nearly halfway to Masúri, at Jeripáni, is a small collection of huts, which may, by a stretch of generosity, be called a village. There is, moreover, here a halfway house where the thirsty traveller might refresh himself by a brandy or whiskey peg, a small bottle of claret, or a cup of tea, whichever might have been his "peculiar vanity;" but alas the old *khansama*, who presided over the destinies of that establishment, is gone, it is hoped, to paradise, and the "resthouse" is in the last stage of decay. Within a few yards of this, on the left, on a knoll close to the road, is a weather-beaten pillar, which, also, is falling into decay. Those who are curious enough to examine this relic may, at its base, see a tablet, which contains the following inscription: - "Sacred to the memory of Sir C. Farrington, *Bart.*, Captain of her Majesty's 35th Regiment, who departed this life on the 28th March 1828, aged 35 years." Nobody ever heard or read anything about Sir C. Farrington and in all probability he was a young Captain, being taken for change to Masúri, with the forefingers of death upon him, but that he could not approach further than this towards his goal. Then we take another turn in the road and another beautiful view of the Dún bursts upon us, but it is for a hundred yards or so only, which bring us into a pretty glade, which leads to the back and front entrances to Fair Lawn. Fair Lawn was, a few years ago, bought by the Sind, Punjab, and Delhi Railway authorities as a summer home and school for the girls of their employés, General Biddulph, by establishing his summer homes for soldiers' children, having set the brilliant example. Further on, and in open view of Masúri proper, we pass under the Manor House estate, with St. George's

College and the St. Fidelis' Orphanage; and, immediately, we reach Barlowgunge, a small village, dominated by Whytbank, that house which looks so much like a castle, as the traveller might have seen it a few minutes before. Here is also that emblem of civilization, the Police *chauki*, which, in its turn, dominates a huge iron water tank, a god-send to man and beast. This tank forms the point at which you, again, have the choice of two roads to Masúri. The selection greatly depends upon the destination of the traveller. All whose destination is eastward of the Kuleri, onwards to the library, and country beyond, can take either without much loss of time. Very few, except those who go to the library and beyond, use the "lower" road, as it is called, and the upper road is most popular. The lower road passes the Crown Brewery, and is in fact the continuation of the Mackinnon road to Rájpur. It is of easy gradient, and more pleasant to travel on. The first point in it, from which the main road, or mall, of Masúri can be reached, is under the Himalaya Hotel, and it is a stiff climb up to the hotel. It then continues on to the library, and there we leave it. The upper road from Barlowgunge has nothing to recommend it but its greater propinquity to Masúri. It is uncomfortably steep from Barlowgunge to Wakefield, but this is not far; but formerly it was agonizing up to the Masúri hotel. A few years ago the Masúri Municipality constructed a road from the Antlers to Sinclair, which cut off the unpleasant "pinch" up to the Masúri Hotel. The worse piece of road remained immediately under "Wayside Cottage," which was incurably rough and rugged, but, thanks again to the Municipality, this wretched and dangerous part has been dismissed from public service, for a new road has been made from the left a little beyond Ralston, which after a steep entrance, runs into a level road to the Antlers, joins the other new way previously mentioned, rising into the familiar and popular road past the Masonic Lodge into Masúri. Still those who are making for the Post Office or Lándaur, must, from the Antlers, take the old acclivity to the Masúri Hotel, and thence along the ancient and imperial highway to Lándaur.

5

Masuri

ASURI is situated in latitude 30° 27' 30"; longitude 78° 6' 30". Banog, the loftiest mountain on the Masúri side of the Himalaya range, attains, according to the Great Trigonometrical Survey map, an elevation of 7,433 feet. As early as the year 1826, the salubrity of the climate, which has a temperature ranging from 27° to 80°, attracted European residents. This of course is technical.

A place like Masúri has no separate history in the strict sense of the term. If it has a history at all, it consists in the rise and progress of stone and mortar. From its splendid situation and easiness of access it is only required to be known to become popular. A place so favoured by nature could not fail to attract when once her beauties were unveiled, and the first house built could only lead to the erection of many more. The great advantage Masúri possesses over other hill-stations is the variety of its scenery. Sanitaria that are far within the hills have but the magnificent snows for us to gaze on, and the bold mountainous region intervening; grand and awe-inspiring, it is true, but, after all, monotonous. The eye tires at looking at those bold prominences, so district in their outline, that you may see them in the dark, as it were, from memory. People, after a short acquaintance with them, rarely give them more than a passing glance, or a good long stare to welcome them after the rains, the cessation of which brings them out of cloudland. At Masúri, however, the crown of the general scenery is the Dehra Dún, backed by the Siwáliks. It forms a panorama of unsurpassed beauty. The eye never tires at looking down upon the Dún, with its multitude of lovely detail, and commanding, as the visitor does, the view from an altitude of from 6,000 to 7,000 feet, the effect is charming, and, under some conditions of the atmosphere, enchanting. Description is beyond the power of the pen.

But we were saying that if Masúri has any history at all, it is the rise and progress of stone and mortar. It certainly has records which chronicle the rise and growth of the station and these are in the Superintendent's office and that of the Survey Department.

It is said that, in 1823, there was only one house in Masúri, now there are more than 300. It is curious to think that the first construction was a small hut built as a shooting-box, on the Camel's Back hill, by Mr Shore and Captain Young in 1823. Being only a shooting-box it can scarcely count as a house, but so it is. Shortly afterwards, another small house is said to have been built, "somewhere about" the Kuleri hill. This is so vague that the archæologist has little chance of turning up the foundations. Mullingar (which, however, is in Lándaur) was about the first house erected, which is recognizable to the present day. In 1827, Government established at Lándaur a convalescent depôt for European soldiers, and it is conjectured that at this time there must have been several houses in Masúri. The Park was built by a Colonel Wyshe about 1827; Phoenix Lodge, in 1829. Building appears to have gone on rapidly; and it is reasonable argued that because a Mr. Lawrence, a merchant, came up with goods for sale in 1829, hutting himself in on the Camel's Back, there must have been a considerable European population. If Mr. Lawrence could pay us a visit at the present time, it would open his eyes to see the number of merchants who now come up with goods. He would retire with shame to think that he was a mere pedlar compared to these.

The advent of beer-brewing, even in Masúri, was as ancient as 1830, when Mr. Bohle, from Meerut, started the old brewery. Two years afterwards, however, he got into trouble about supplying beer to soldiers who presented forged passes. Colonel Young appears to have been both Superintendent of the Dun and commandant of Landaur. It looks very much like the old antipathy between officials and outsiders, for we find Mr. Bohle was called to account by Colonel Young for distilling spirits without a license, but though Mr. Bohle certainly distilled whiskey at Meerut, there is no record or trace of a distillery in Masúri. However Mr. Bohle closed the concern and sold the estate to a Mr. Parsons in 1832.

In the same year Colonel Everest, the then Surveyor-General opened an office at the Park, and made an almost level road to it, which still exists as an example of his scientific skill.

These are many reasons for coming to the conclusion that Masúri was to have been in the direction of Hatipaon and

Cloud End. Masuri and Landaur were in those days entirely distinct and separated by a considerable distance.

In the earlier history of Masuri, European settlers took up their land under direct agreements with the village *zemindars* on both slopes of the hills. In reference to these northern and southern slopes a curious boundary question has arisen. The boundary line between the Dehra Dun District and the territories left to Sudershan Sah, the Raja of Tehri, who was reinstated after the British had driven out the Ghurkas, was the watershed line of the Masuri and Landaur range. This question was first discussed when the convalescent depôt was established in Landaur. It appears from the correspondence on the subject that the acknowledged boundary line was, as abovementioned, the crest or ridge dividing the south-western from the north-eastern watershed of the lower Himalayan range; consequently, those portions of Masuri and Landaur on the northern slopes of the hills are not in British territory. Compensations were accordingly fixed to be paid both by the Masuri Municipality and Landaur to the Tehri Raja for land appropriated northward of the ridge. As more land is taken up additional compensation is given. Of course, this involved the question of the jurisdiction of the British Courts, but the authorities made short work of objections of this sort.

In 1834, Mr. Mackinnon comes upon the scene, and Masuri owes a good deal to his energy and public spirit. He bought Mr. Bohle's former estate, and opened a school called the Masúri Seminary. Mr. Bohle also returned and recommenced brewing, and afterwards built the place known as Bohle's brewery, now in ruins, to the north.

In 1835, the European population felt strong enough to build a Church, and after some discussion regarding the site, the result was that the nave and tower of the present church was built in 1836. A Bank, called the "North-West Bank," was floated, but it came to grief in 1842. The present branch of the Delhi and London Bank was opened in 1859; and in 1864, the Mussoorie Savings Bank was started. The Mussoorie Bank, now in existence, is identical except in name. In 1874, the Himalaya Bank was started by Mr. F. Moss, and has made such progress as to render it a firmly established institution.

Before Dhulip Singh, the son of Runjit Singh, went to England to be educated and trained under English auspices, he occupied the "Castle" in Masuri, the property of Mr. G. B. Taylor, and it is well known that the ex-Amir Yakub Khan resides in Masuri, which, doubtless, he finds a prison inflicting the mildest possible discomfort. At Belle Vue he has a large retinue to minister to his wants and his pleasures, and as he is permitted to ride about the station at will – a privilege of which he takes abundant advantage – the fetters which blind him to Masuri and Dehra must be loose and easy.

The Himalaya Club, one of the best in India, furnishes reminiscences which form part of the history of Masuri. It was established in 1841, and its organization was in a great measure due to Lieutenant (now General) Showes. The Club now has on its books 759 members. To accommodate the large increase of resident members, the building has been very largely expanded, and forms a prominent object of observation from most points in Masuri and Landaur.

The Newspaper Press, too, found a home in Masuri long before any other hill-station dreamt of a journal. Mr. Mackinnon gave birth to "The Hills" in 1842, and with the assistance of able writers, who were all somewhat radical, kept it afloat about eight years, supported by a good circulation. Ten years afterwards "The Hills" was "born again" in a more expanded shape, but it finally succumbed to fate in 1865. Afterwards, about 1870, a "Mussoorie Exchange Advertiser" made its appearance, but, as its title implies, was mainly a medium for advertisements. The "Mussoorie Season," launched by the late Mr. Coleman in 1872, although it sometimes possessed a tendency to give needless offence, the management was by no means void of ability. The Proprietor left India in September 1874, and after the end of the season, the "Mussoorie Season" ceased to exist in its former shape. At the commencement of the following season (1875), the "Himalaya Chronicle" (with which was incorporated the "Mussoorie Season") was started by the present writer, and therefore he does not permit himself to say more than that the journal is in the tenth year of its existence. It is intended to continue the publication of the "Himalaya Chronicle" all the year round, and the number of its columns is to be increased. It advocates the claims of the landed interest as well as those of non-official Europeans and of planters and independent Europeans and natives, who invest their capital in the development of new Industries. It has, for advertisers, a guaranteed circulation of not less than 500 copies twice a week, proved by certificate of the local postmaster. From the same press, too, is published "The Chameleon," an advertiser for all India, with a guaranteed circulation of 1,000. The announcement, moreover, is made that, at the "Himalaya Chronicle" Press, there will be published a "Civil, Military and Commercial Guide," somewhat after the style of David's "Guide," once so popular, but now discontinued. Such a work, which is to be published quarterly, has been much in request, and should be a very useful publication, and lowly priced at Rs. 2, including all expense of transmission. The "Hills Advertiser," published by Messrs. Buckle and Co., is freely distributed by post locally. It made its appearance, first, solely as a medium for advertisements, but now gives scraps of local news, which, of course, impart additional interest to the publication.

❦❦❦

PANORAMA OF MASURI.

Entering the Sanitarium from either of the roads previously mentioned, the visitor arrives at points from which the whole southern face of the settlement bursts upon his view. Of course, a more distant perspective is obtained from Dehra, and even from Asaruri. The houses are plainly visible from the most distant points, crowning the ridges and nestling on the sides of the precipices. But, say, a little beyond Jari Pani, the view of the station is magnificent. Masuri seems to be perched upon the summit of the inner semicircle of a leviathan amphitheatre, a huge cul de sac, formed by the mountain spurs which run down to the Dehra Valley. After Barlowgunge, very little is seen of Masuri until one gets well into the station and underneath the Himalaya Hotel. Here a capital view of the central Dun can be obtained. On the left to the east the Manor House Estate stands out boldly prominent, backed by the Himalayan spurs eastward; also, lower down, Fair Lawn, the summer sanitarium of the children of the employés of the S. P. and D. Railway, a Brobdignagian spur running from it down to the Rajpur side of the Dun. Nearer, but still to the left, is the important village of Batta; nearer still to the right, one can look down upon the more important village of Kiarkulim both being flanked and surrounded by the terraced patches of cultivation on the sloping hillsides so familiar to hill-travellers. To the west rises Vincent's Hill, above which rises "Hill Top," on part of Blucher's Hill, with a large spur running down below the Batta Falls. To the south of "Hill Top" is "Belle Vue," the residence of ex-Amir Yakub Khan, nestling on the north side of a hillock on the spur which obscures the house from the south. Under "Hill Top" and to the right is Waverley Hill, which is well wooded, and dominated by that splendid-looking building, the Convent. Here also the Masuri Library may be seen, with the Masuri School, with its little Church, above and behind it. As you go along the Mall from the east, you are, in the early morning, within the shadow of the Camel's Back Hill to the right; in the evening you would have to face the blinding westward sun. Far down below the Mall that ample building is Caineville House School for Girls. From this point of view, Christ's Church, the Church of Masuri, is hidden, but by going through the little Masuri bazaar and on to the Library, a good view of the Church and the buildings on the western side of the Camel's Back can be obtained. Masuri occasionally makes spasmodic efforts to get up a band, and when it does meet with success, which is always very short-lived, the band plays at this spot, - *i.e.*, in front of the Library, which is a very popular lounge and a *rendezvous* for those who live on the further side of Masuri.

Returning towards the Church, we come upon the narrow gorge, which leads to the Camel's Back Road, a popular walk or ride on account of its being almost completely level. A little way in from the gorge, another fine view of the well-wooded Waverley Hill may be obtained; on the left "Hill-Top" again, and to the right the principal houses of the Happy Valley Estate high up over the Chakrata and Simla Road. Further on, and taking a seat at "Scandal! Point," which is a small promontory running off from the road, Benog, a very high hill to the west, may be seen jutting up into the sky between a dip formed by the north side of Waverley and the south of the hill forming the eastern part of the Happy Valley Estate. Looking down the deep *khud* at your feet, you catch a glimpse of the deep valley through which the Aglar River runs, the hills descending to which being fruitful of vegetation, the villages and terraced fields on either sides and round about the Nag Tiba Range being very pretty to look at. The Nag Tiba Range is immediately across the Aglar, and at proper seasons is the haunt of the sportsman. All along the slopes of the hills the land looks quite bare, and every year the villagers set fire to the undergrowth, in order to prepare the soil for cultivation. Nag Tiba itself may

be reached either by the Tehri Road or up the valley of the Aglar. A portion of the snowy range is seen from the Camel's Back Road, but much is hidden from view by the Nag Tiba Hills forming part of the Tyne Range. The patch of green we see in the distance to our left front is Chakrata, and with a good glass the buildings are plainly discernible. Further on is Deoband, and to the left is the great Chur Mountain, within the territory of the Rajah of Sirmur. We will leave "Scandal Point," and proceed on the Camel's Back Road. About two hundred yards ahead is a spot where, tradition says, a lady on horseback exhibited considerable courage and presence of mind. The rains had washed away a small bridge which covered a fearful chasm. Approaching this at a canter, she did not observe the gap until close on to it, too late to pull up, but she suddenly quickened her horse's pace and cleared the interspace. From this spot we are now facing Fern Hill and Cottage, the road under which is beautifully cool in the hottest time of the season. On one spot for some distance the sun never shines. We now proceed on our walk to the Cemetery. Here we can have a fine view of the Landaur Hill, with its huge spur sloping down into the Aglar Valley. About thirty yards before reaching the rustic entrance to Kirklands, if the visitor will look up to the top of the Camel's Back Hill, he will see an almost perfect natural statue in rock of a camel crouched down on his knees and haunches, laden to the full. This small piece of rock, so fashioned in nature's own mould, gave, they say, the hill on which it rests the name it bears. One thing in favour of the idea is, that from no aspect can the general appearance of the hill be likened to a camel's back. A few yards further on eastward is the shooting range of the Masuri Volunteer Rifle Corps, at the 500 yards firing point, that being the longest distance available in such an awkward country. The targets are down low underneath the more ancient part of the Cemetery. We continue our way, we round the northern and eastern sides of Zephyr Hill, and are in sight of the Kuleri Bazaar. Besides Landaur, as has been before mentioned, we have a close view of the western face of the Castle Hill Estate, dominated by the Castle itself, including the pretty little Church of All Saints. Closer, and to the right front, we see the Union Church, the Municipal Hall and Club, Post Office, together with some private houses. Now, we are again on the Mall, at the bottom of the Kuleri Hill and Bazaar. We ascend the hill to the Delhi and London and Himalaya Banks, descend past the Masuri Bank, the Himalaya Chronicle Press, the Himalaya Hotel, down to the point whence we started. This neighbourhood, thickly built on, is really the heart of Masuri, the business centre par excellence. We will now turn to the left from the exit from the Camel's Back Road

and ascend the hill to the Post Office. There is really little to see along this road that has not been already mentioned, except a better view of the Camel's Back skirted by its now excellent road, and a sight of the eastern face of Zephyr Hill, with its cluster of houses, which look picturesque when bathed in the morning sunlight. When we arrive at the Post Office we are at the Ultima Thule of the eastern part of Masuri, and Landaur Bazaar is hitched on to it without a break, not even so much as that which divides two railway carriages. Now, we will return through the whole length and breadth of the Mall to the Library – a distance of about two miles. After reaching our initial point of observation under the Himalaya Hotel, the Mall, with the exception of a slight rise passing Knockane, is, to the Library, almost as level as a billiard table. We take the road to the left of the Library, "Blucher's Hill Road", and proceed at once over Vincent's Hill to Blucher's Hill, and sitting upon one of the numerous crags which crown the hill, a feast of the most charming scenery is open to us. A small binocular is a great luxury at such a place as this. On a clear day we here command an almost complete view of the Dehra Dun. Looking due south the eye rests upon Dehra itself, with its white houses peeping out of the ample foliage. A little to the west of Dehra may be seen a cluster of tea gardens, with their white walls reflecting the strong light of the sun.

The source of the Tans *naddi* is almost at your feet among the spurs below, and as it expands on reaching the valley, it can be traced running into the Asan *naddi*, a little way from Jhajra, and which *naddi* runs westward into the Jamna. To the left are the great eastern spurs, over the abrupt outline of which the sun rises as with a bound. Straight ahead runs the long chain of the Siwaliks, which looks insignificant from our standpoint, and which we look down upon from the altitude of Blucher's Hill. We are perched too high for the Siwaliks to obscure a view of the plains of the Saharanpur District, and during a break in the rains, every detail stands out with marvellous clearness. To the right front, the sacred Jamna can be seen, like a broad silver line, dividing the Umballa District from that of Saharanpur, pursuing its course onward to its destination. To the left front the broad bosom of the holy Ganges is traceable to the verge of the horizon, as it takes its initial course plain-wards to the Sandarbands. Just over the Siwaliks, south-east, a great patch may be seen; that is Rurki. With a good glass, Saharanpur has been plainly distinguished. In fact, it is impossible to adequately describe this lovely view, and no word-painting can sufficiently sketch the multiplicity of its detail.

The writer, in the early morning in the middle of July, went to the summit of Blucher's Hill, with binoculars in hand, in the hope of refreshing his memory by a good long look at this exquisitely charming panorama. He was glad to be disappointed, for he was more than compensated by the view of a composite piece of scenery which one seldom has the opportunity of enjoying. Huge fleecy clouds having all the density of *cumuli* had risen from the valley and the lower spurs beneath. Patches of the valley might be seen here and there, but the Dun was practically obscured fro all purposes of observation. At Masuri we are sometimes within, and sometimes literally above, the clouds, which are casting their shadows on the Dun and plains below. On the occasion in question, the Siwaliks were covered by a similarly white mantle, and smaller cloudlets dappled the sylvan slopes that flank the range. As the nearer clouds imperceptibly rose, patches of the valley, bathed in sunlight, became visible. The curtain was frequently lifted over the Dun, discovering it, as it were, by fascinating installments, miles at a time. As the sun throws out its heat, these mountains of wool-like clouds dissolve into mist, which pours into Masuri with such unpleasant effect.

If the day is clear, face about and you enjoy a splendid view of the snowy range with its gigantic details. The Nag Tiba Hills still hide a portion of them, but from Vincent's Hill and Blucher's Hill in close proximity, one of the best views of the snows, within the proper precincts of Masuri, may be obtained. Of Landaur, hereafter. In the vicinity of Cloud End, perhaps, a better point may be obtained, but one has to go some four or five miles to get it.

⋈⋈⋈⋈

WALKS AND RIDES.

For the horseman or the pedestrian, Masuri furnishes all that can reasonably be required. Of course, the Mall from the Post Office to the Library is pre-eminently in the front rank, but, par excellence, from beneath the Himalaya Hotel to the Library. It is mainly here that ladies and gentlemen indulge in that furious riding which is so strictly prohibited on magisterial authority, and pedestrians who do not nourish a wish to be galloped over, or blinded with dust, seek quieter roads for their perambulations. The Camel's Back Road is popular with pedestrians, and it is now kept in excellent order. It is also patronized by those on horseback. It takes about three-quarters of an hour to walk completely round the Camel's Back Road, but it is a very enjoyable "constitutional" if taken in the early morning, or in the twilight of the evening. One not only catches glimpses of the snows, but the hill scenery is very pretty, extending into the Sirmur territory, dominated by the Great Chur mountain. From the Library there is an excellent ride or walk, quite level to the gate of the Charleville Hotel. By turning into the Tallahmur Road there is a capital bridle and foot path, with a slight gradient, up to the convent. Along this road a capital view of Benog can be had, and the nearer scenery downwards to the right is very pretty. If the rider or walker chooses to extend his explorations of the highways and byeways of Masuri, he might turn to the right, when arriving at the Convent, and continue on the main road, past the Botanical Gardens, towards the Old (Mackinnon's) Brewery, until arriving at the entrance to, and striking into, the Everest Road, which is level and pleasant to "The Park" gates. If still further curious, he might continue on up-hill to Cloud End. Returning thence, he might take the upper road, near the Botanical Gardens, which leads to Vincent's Hill, and down the Blucher's Hill Road to the Library; or if he goes no further than the convent, he has the option of striking the Blucher's Hill road a few hundred yards further down, or taking the shorter cut, to the left, down a shady path, to the Happy Valley road, north of Masuri School, a short distance from the Library. Down and up the Mackinnon's Road past the Crown Brewery and back is quite a rural pathway. For the sake of variety, the rider or walker might circumambulate the tank at Barlowgunge and return by way of the Antlers, taking the well-frequented road which leads past the Masonic Hall, or, as an alternative, take the upper path leading past the Masuri Hotel up to the Post Office. Near Kingcraig on the Mackinnon's Road there is a seldom-used path, of easy gradient, leading up to Clairville, where it runs into the Masonic Lodge Road. A pleasant walk may be had around the Castle Hill. A few years ago, there was great promise of a good ride or walk round Vincent's Hill. From the Blucher's Hill Road the Vincent's Hill Road branches off to the left under the south side of the Masuri School. The constant slips that occur under "Charlemont" renders it difficult to keep the road fit for any traffic. Some few years ago, the Municipality spent a good round sum of money to construct this road round and beyond "Frosty Hall" into the Mackinnon's Road, just below the Botanical Gardens, a distance of about two miles, but for some unexplainable reason abandoned it, so that for horses it is now impassable, and pedestrians even have one, two, or three points to make hops, skips and jumps, over nasty places. When the term "abandoned" is used, it is not meant that the road will never be put in order and railed in; when it is, it will form one of the best rides and walks in Masuri. These are the main walks and rides in the Sanatarium, but there are abundant opportunities, especially for the pedestrian, to seek and find peripatetic pastures new.

PICNIC AND PLEASURE RESORTS.

Taking the more distant and least easy of access we commence with:-

BANOG. – A party should start early in the morning if they wish to enjoy a trip to Banog. It is 7,400 feet above the level of the sea, and is bare of every kind of vegetation except a coarse kind of grass on which cattle browse with satisfaction. Strike into the Everest Road as before mentioned, up the hill to a little this side of Cloud End, when a downward path is struck to the foot of Banog. A little more than half way up the hill is the ruins of an old house, and a grove to trees, under which the creature comforts of a picnic are partaken. It is very unsatisfactory journey if you don't surmount the summit, near the old G. T. Survey Observatory, now in ruins. Here the eye can feast on a fine view of the snowy range, and a pretty look-down on the Simla and Chakrata Road below the Kempti Falls. Parties should not loiter longer than 4 p.m., as the distance is seven miles to the Banks, even.

AGLAR RIVER AND VALLEY.– This cannot be called a picnic place, and only in a genial moment a pleasure resort. A pious traveller in England, writing home at the conclusion of a long journey said, he had arrived at a certain point "by the blessing of God and a strong pair of boots." Any pious gentlemen, 'doing' the Aglar from Masuri and back in a day, might reproduce this quaint expression, and something more, for healthy lungs and strong and firm muscles are as much required as the holy blessing and the strong boots. There are may *pag-dandis* from various points leading down to the river, but the best is acknowledged to be that on the Simla and Chakrata Road, which runs down by the side of a hillock, on which is perched what may be a temple, a boundary pillar, or any nameless thing, but in reality is a store-house for the telegraph wires. Four-legged ponies have to be left at this point. A dandi is reputed to be capable of landing one in the valley, and probably a light weight would run little risk of being dropped or tilted over; but Shanks' pony, two-legged, is much more safe to a good hill-walker. Some sport, both in shooting and fishing, may be obtained at proper seasons, and also a good swim in some of the pools. One has to start early in the afternoon to get home before dark, not later than 3 p.m., and even earlier if there be a party among whom there are those who always lag behind.

KEMPTI FALLS. – These are over six miles from the aforesaid heart of Masuri. The Ringaul Naddi supplies the water, and, being the largest falls in or about Masuri, have a very imposing appearance from the Chakrata Road. Being an imperial road, it is good travelling all down to a little past Kempti Village, but the path is very steep down to the foot of the falls, although dandies and jhampans can now descend. A good hill-pony, too, is quite safe, especially in coming up. There are five separate falls, all running straight down into one another, aggregating about 600 feet altogether. According to the G. T. Survey Map, the crown of the topmost fall is 4,680 feet, that of the lowest 4,120 feet, above sea level. By leaving at 4 p.m., Masuri may be comfortably reached by dark. A short cut from the Happy Valley to Kempti should be avoided; in fact, short cuts generally should. The writer is in a position to speak from bitter experience.

BATTA FALLS. – As the Mackinnon's road is now-a-days in good order, the best approach to these falls is by that road to Batta Village, through the village, over some cultivated land, to a point where ponies have to be left. Empty dandies might be taken down to the falls for convenience' sake, but it would be a hazardous matter to occupy them. As the falls are neared, there are some awkward banks for ladies, and down which one has to slither, but there is little or no danger to be apprehended from them. The falls are very pretty, and their distinguishing feature is the many charming and picturesque little nooks that may be found all along the banks of the *naddi* (Kiarkuli Naddi), and which may be got at by a little exploration. By crossing the *naddi* – a very easy matter – and proceeding down stream, some pretty spots may be reached. From the Caineville School a spur of easy gradient will lead to the falls, but this is an approach for men and boys to gratify curiosity or to indulge in sport. There is a tolerably decent road to the Batta Village from Barlowgunge, but since the Mackinnon's Road has been put in order, it is seldom or never used.

HARDY FALLS. – The locality of these can hardly be called a place for picnics or a pleasure resort. They are approached from the south-western spurs from Vincent's Hill. They are only visited by men and boys out for a day's constitutional or for sport. The distance from Masuri forms a bar to their being visited except on rare occasions.

MURRAY FALLS. – These falls, also, are very difficult of approach, and the real falls can only be reached by the adventurous. A good road past Midlands and on to Dhobi Ghat, south of the Landaur Hill, offers considerable advantages for part of the way. Beyond this, for a longway, the ground offers few obstacles, and descending further down, there is an easy *pag-dandi*, but when the *naddi* is reached, the pedestrian's difficulties commence. By perseverance, however, the view of the falls may be obtained. Just below the falls a smaller stream from above

discharges itself over a precipice, 150 feet in height, into the *naddi* below. This presents a fine sight during the rains, but few would care to risk the perils of the monsoon on such a journey. In the driver seasons, this fall is hardly worth looking at, there being only a driblet of water to run over it. The *naddi*, running down to the foot of the hill, finally reaches the Sulphur Springs, Sahasradara, or Thousand Drippings. To reach these springs by way of the *naddi* is impossible. The only way to reach them is viâ Rajpur, the Raspanna must be crossed, either by the mill close under Rajpur, or about half-a-mile down stream. The latter is the more convenient for ponies, as the other route offers a few obstacles. There is no regular road, but along the pathway the ground is ornamented by some picturesque mangoe topes. Either way the village of Nagal must be passed through; after this there is a nasty descent, but by no means dangerous, into the dry bed of what in the rains is a mountain stream running into the Ganges, a short distance through some low jungle, and we come upon the springs. The petrifying cave may be reached without much difficulty, and within are indeed the Thousand Drippings, so that an umbrella might be found a convenient article, the sulphur water oozes from the hill-side and petrifies every solid thing with which it comes in contact. Twigs of trees, fern leaves, chicken bones, all become encrusted with lime and sulphur, and numerous specimens are easily procured and brought away. Numerous stalactites hand from the roof of the cave, assuming the form of icicles, produced, of course, by the deposit of the metallic bases of the water. On the floor of the cavern is that deposit of earthy or calcareous matter, formed by the drops, and technically known as stalagmite. On the other side of the stream is a sulphur spring, which oozes from the ground, and which also possesses petrifying powers. Some dispute the statement that these are petrifactions, but say they are simply encrustations of lime or whatever the metallic bases may be which cause the curious phenomena. That is a question which must be left to the scientific, but it is one worth solving. At the spot where these springs are to be found, there is nothing else to interest the visitor, for it is a dismal wilderness. The Murray Falls and these springs were discovered by Dr. Murray more than thirty years ago. Dr. Murray had some huts built near these springs, and sent a number of ailing soldiers from the Landaur Depôt to benefit by what he considered the healing powers of these waters; but the experiment was not pursued.

THE BOTANICAL GARDENS. – These are the most easy of access from Masuri Proper, and are about two miles from the Banks. There are two roads to them from the Library; the one to the right branching off from the Happy Valley road under the Masuri School to the Convent Gate. A short distance down the Mackinnon's Road, the entrance will be found to the right. They have been used by the Government as experimental gardens, but the Government having fixed upon another spot to the south-east of Masuri and announced a year ago that the gardens under mention would be put up to auction. The Masuri Municipality, however, arranged to buy the gardens for Rs. 10,000, and the auction-sale was countermanded. It is satisfactory to find that this popular place of resort is not to be split up into lots and sold to the highest bidder. These gardens possess the advantage of being near. There is a small summer-house for shelter in case of rain, a badminton ground, prettily laid out parterres of flowers, and groves of fruit trees. If there be any disadvantage at all, it lies in the fact that they are always open to the public, and as their proximity renders them liable to a constant flow of visitors, a party cannot obtain that privacy which most people like when indulging in the frolics of a picnic.

THE HAPPY VALLEY. – This spot is also very easy of access. A level road all the way to the gate-way, which shows the way to the Charleville Hotel and many of the houses on the Happy Valley estate. From this point there is an easy descent to the valley where there is the most extensive plateau in or near the station. It is not so much a picnic ground as a pleasure resort. Here cricket matches take place, gymkanas are held, with a small race-course round which riders manage to steer their horses with few or no accidents, athletic sports take place, horse and dog shows are held, where important volunteer parades muster, and the annual inspection occur; in fact, the Happy Valley is the only place where anything big can find room. There are also a billiard-room, a bijou theatre, and, generally speaking, the place is par excellence, the one for great *tamashas*. The distance is about two and-a-half miles from the banks.

JABARKET. – This is a spot approached by the Tehri Road, between three and four miles from Masuri. A little beyond the Bunniah's shops, a pathway to the left leads up to a rather extensive plateau for the hills, and forms a very pleasant resort for picnics. There is plenty of room for a good foot-race, and the scenery around, from most points, magnificent. Ponies, jhampans and dandies can go up all the way.

TIVOLI GARDENS. – These gardens were opened in May 1882, and at once became a favorite resort of the Masuri public. They are situated about one mile and-a-half from the banks, in the direction of Barlowgunge. On leaving the main highway opposite Ralston, one immediately enters a shady and tortuous road, which leads to the gardens. The first view of Tivoli is a dancing pavilion,

with dressing-rooms, a dining saloon, with cookroom attached, and beds of choice flowers are prettily laid out. Lower down are tennis and badminton courts in good order, and again below, there are fruit trees and beds of strawberries. The road then leads to the stream with its numerous waterfalls, the principal of them being named the "Mossy Falls," the "Hearsey Falls," &c. Along the banks are summer houses and pretty nooks for picnics, such as the Fairy's Glen, &c. The path by the stream is in good order, and ample for conveyance of elderly and portly chaperones, while such a place as the Cupid's Bower is only accessible to those who discover that the "course of true love never did run smooth."

THE PARK. – This used to be a favorite place of resort, but as the house has been occupied, it ceases to be available.

SNOWY RANGE. – To this section of the present book it may be added that the nearest places for views of the Snowy Range are Vincent's Hill and Blucher's Hill. From the latter, a splendid view of the Dehra Dun also may be obtained. The view of the snows is even better from Lal Tiba, and the piece of ground above the Roman Catholic Chapel, both at Landaur. At either place, the grand peak called the Bandar Punch, looking like a leviathan double-poled tent, may be seen; also the

Siri Kanta, apparently leaning on one side like the tower of Pisa; also the long succession of peaks to the east of the latter. But for an uninterrupted view, the traveller should descend into the Algar Valley, and then proceed onwards to the village of Mararah (Ballu being the usual camping ground), and on the top of the hill between Mararah and Lalauri a connected view of the Snowy Range may be obtained. It is two or three marches out, and therefore, a tent and camping requisites are necessary.

ᘓᘓᘓᘓᘓ

INSTITUTIONS OF MASURI.

MUNICIPAL COMMITTEE. – A Municipal Committee was established so long ago as 1842. The functions of the Committee, at present, are to look after the sanitation of the settlement, to regulate and control the building of houses and all matters that may conduce to the convenience and welfare of the residents. They have power to levy certain taxes or cesses, both against proprietors and tenants. Their duty also is to dispense the funds and generally to regulate and control the finances of the municipal system. The Committee numbers twelve members, a proportion of whom are ex-officio. The majority represent the proprietors, the minority the tenants. An elected member holds office for three years, but is open to re-election. The Municipal Hall belongs to the Committee. It is the common resort for all theatrical entertainments, balls, fancy fairs, public meetings, &c., &c. It has recently been considerably enlarged at great expense, but the hall is so constantly occupied, that the whole outlay will be recouped at an early date. When this is accomplished, the hall will form a handsome source of income to the Committee. The following details of the income and expenditure of the municipality may be interesting: - The tax on houses, buildings, and lands for the year 1882-3 to March 31 – cess collection, Rs. 9,907-6-5; tenants' tax, 7,238-15-9; site tax or ground rent, Rs. 2,644-9-0 (Rs 1,120, or thereabout being paid to zemindars, owners of land); hall rents for entertainments, &c., Rs. 2,220; quarters for Sergeant Instructor of Volunteers, Rs. 280; tolls on animals, &c., passing through Rajpur toll-bar, under contracts, Rs. 9,600; other items swell these figures up to a grand total of income of Rs. 34,008-0-6. The expenditure shows the following items: - Original works, including watersupply works, new diversion of road under Ralston, jhampan sheds, & c., Rs. 3,780-12-5; repairs of roads, pushtas, & c., Rs. 8,569-13-6; hall improvement, Rs. 2,610-9-4; conservancy, Rs. 6,708-11-3; to cantonment funds, one-tenth of tolls, Rs. 960; other items render the grand total of expenditure to Rs. 34,429-5-11. The Superintendent of the Dun, Mr. W. Church, C. S., is now the President;

Mr. H. G. Scott, the Vice President; the other members are General Angelo, Mr. T. W. Fitch, Mr. G. Hunter, Revd. A. Stokes, Messrs. C. F. Stowell, J. W. Whymper and Lalla Ramnomund. This is one less than the proper complement, Dr. Pringle, and elected member having gone to England. The District Superintendent of Police, (now Col. Bramley) and the Civil Surgeon (now Dr. Gardner), act as ex-officio members, but the new Municipal Law has considerably curtailed the functions of Government ex-officio members. There are 340 European houses and 140 native houses in Masuri, according to municipal records.

HIMALAYA CLUB. – This Club was organized on its original status in 1841. The present trustees are Mr. Wilmot Lane, C. S., Revd. A. Stokes, M. A., and Lieut. – Col. H. B. Sanderson. The House Committee stands as follows: - Major G. M. B. Hornsby, R. A., Col. H. R. Wintle, Major W. J. Heaviside, R. E., Dr. R. Reid, Hon'ble M. G. Talbot, R. E., and Mr. R. A. Wahab, R. E. The Secretary is Mr. F. B. Simons. The number of members are made up as follows: - Temporary members under Rule IX, 258; members residing in India other than in the Presidencies of Bombay or Madras, 224; members absent from India or in the Presidencies of Bombay or Madras, 277; total, 759. Rule IX provides for the admission by ballot of temporary members, who pay a donation of Rs. 50 for the season, or Rs. 16 for two months, but who have no voice in the management of the Club, no power of voting, nor privilege of claiming honorary membership with other Clubs. It may be useful for visitors to be acquainted with the following abstract of the rules for election and admission of members:

1. Every candidate must be proposed by one member, and seconded by another. Ballot open only between 15th April and 15th October. No candidate admissible for ballot more than twice.

2. Candidate's name, rank, profession or occupation, with name of his proposer and seconder, entered in Secretary's register, and also place on notice board in Club dining-room, at least ten days before ballot. Committee of management appoint the day for ballot.

3. No ballot is valid unless 12 members vote; one black ball in six excludes a candidate.

4. Ballot boxes to be opened in the presence of one or more members of the Committee of Management, who shall record the result in the Register thus, "candidate elected" or the reverse; but the presence of black balls shall on no account be disclosed.

5. Candidates who have been duly proposed and seconded may, on the responsibility of proposer and seconder, be permitted to take rooms in the

Club, pending result of the ballot.

6. No person who has been dismissed from her Majesty's service is eligible for election as a member of the Club.

Candidates, on election, will be supplied with a copy of the Club Rules.

There are 32 suites of rooms, 8 suites having been recently added.

MASURI VOLUNTEER RIFLE CORPS.

– This Corps was raised in 1871. It was kept up with tolerable spirit for some time, but gradually languished until 1877, when the formation of A, or the Station Company, revived an institution which was almost defunct. There are now four companies; A, the Station Company; B, the Masuri School Cadet Company; C, the St. Georges' College Cadet Company; and D, the Dehra Company, The Commissioned Officers of the Corps are, Major Wilmot Lane, C. S., Commandant; Captain E. A. Wainwright, H. G. Scott, C. F. Stowell; Lieutenants C. F. Hamer, J. W. Whymper, F. Todd, H. W. Loof, J. Sheehan, and E. A. Murphy.

The strength of the Corps up to date is as follows:-

Officers, 10; Non-Commissioned Officers, 17; Volunteers, 174; Grand total, 201. The following is the number of extra-efficients, efficients, and no-efficients in 1882:-

Extra-efficients	Efficients	Non-efficients	Total
146	53	3	202

THE MASURI LIBRARY. - This Library was instituted in 1843. It is situated on the open piece of ground, under the Masuri School, where it is flanked on either side by the commencement of the Blucher's Hill and Happy Valley roads. All the newest periodicals and newspapers are taken in, and the shelves are stocked with books of every shade of literature. The Library forms a first class lounge, and it is a rendezvous where people meet either for gossip, or for company with those who reside beyond it. The Literary and Reading-room are governed by the following Rules:-

1. All payments to be made in advance. No name can be entered or retained upon the books until payment is made or renewed, nor can any book be issued to a person until his name has been entered as a subscriber and a ticket of admission has been given to him. No one shall be allowed the use of the Library or Reading-room after the term of subscription has expired.

A Subscriber's book shall be kept on one of the tablets of her Library, and it shall be the duty of each Subscriber to enter his [or her] name therein; and further on sign his [or her] name on the counterfoil of the printed receipt.

To Subscribers of periods of not less than three months, a notice will be issued a week before the expiry of their subscription.

2. The following are the rates of subscriptions:-

	Single	Family
	Rs. As. P.	Rs. As. P.
For 1 week	2 0 0	3 0 0
" 2 "	3 0 0	4 0 0
" 1 Month	5 0 0	7 0 0
" 2 "	9 0 0	12 0 0
" 3 "	12 0 0	16 0 0
" 6 "	24 0 0	32 0 0
" 12 "	36 0 0	48 0 0

A family subscription admits to the use of Reading-room all relatives permanently co-resident with the Subscriber; but allows only three works to be taken out at a time.

A resident Tutor or Governess in a Subscriber's family is admitted to the use of the Reading-room on payment of Rs. 12 [Twelve] per annum.

A single subscription admits the Subscriber only.

The Subscriber only shall be allowed to vote at the General Meetings, or to serve on the Committee.

Every Subscriber shall be furnished with a copy of the Rules before his name is entered on the book.

MASONIC LODGES. – Lodge "Dalhousie," situated below, and to the south of the Himalaya Club, on the road from the Kuleri to the Masuri Hotel, and now called the "Masonic Lodge Road," was constituted under warrant of the Grand Master, August 32 st, 1845. The first Master was the Revd. T. Cartwright Smythe; Col. – Waugh, Surveyor General of India, being the first Senior Warden, and Mr. R. Berrill, first Junior Warden. The original number of the Lodge was 422; it is now No. 639 E. C. The meetings are now held on the first and third Mondays of each month. The present Wor. Master is Wor. Bro. T. W. Fitch.

There is a Royal Arch Chapter, "St. John the Baptist," attached to the Lodge, which was formed, in November 1855, by the Revd. T. C. Smythe, W. R. Ford, Esq., and Major J. Abercrombie. The present principal Z. is Wor. Bro. V. A. Mackinnon.

There is also a Mark Lodge, 'Adoniram,' constituted in 1875. The present Wor. Master is Wor. Brother F. B. Simons.

Ledge 'Caledonia,' under the Scotch constitution, was formed in 1881, the first Master being Wro. Brother F. H. Treherne, followed last year by Wor. Brother B. J. White. The present Master is Wor. Brother W. C. Hurst. This lodge first held its meetings at 'Mayfield,' near the Union Chapel, but last year removed to "The Glen."

SUMMER HOME FOR SOLDIERS' CHILDREN. – This is a nobly charitable and most deserving institution, and provides for the advantages of a hill climate for the children of soldiers to the extent of 100. The Home is at 'Glenburnie,' underneath the Botanical Gardens, and was established in 1876, under the auspices of General Biddulph. During the seven years of its existence, from 1876 to 1882 inclusive, 488 children have been admitted, and four deaths occurred during that period. The progress of the Home has been most rapid. The roll of children accommodated in 1876 contained only 44 children; in 1882, 48 boys and 39 girls were received into the house; a considerable proportion arriving in delicate and precarious health, and leaving at the close of the season in vigorous health and spirits. The Home is supported by voluntary donations and subscriptions, amateur theatricals, entertainments, concerts, church offertories, fees paid by parents, & c., &c. The patrons are H. E. The Most Noble the Marquis of Ripon, K. G., P. C., G.M.SI., Viceroy and Governor General of India; H. E. General Sir D. M. Stewart, Bart., G.C.B., C.I.E., Commander-in-Chief in India; The Hon'ble Sir C. Aitchision, K.C.S.I., Lieut.-Governor of the Punjab and its Dependencies. The patronesses are the Marchioness of Ripon, Lady Stewart, and Lady Aitchison. The Local Committee of Management at Masuri are: - President, the General Officer commanding the Division; Members, the Superintendent of the Dun, the Commandant of Landaur Depôt, the Chaplain of Masuri, and the Civil Surgeon of Masuri. The Lady Superintendent is Mrs Chapman.

The Summer Home opens annually in April, when (100) one hundred children can be admitted for the hot months, the season ending about the first week in November. The object of this Institution is to benefit the children of soldiers serving in India, by removing the weakly and suffering for a season or so from the effects of the heat of the plains. Tuition (mental and industrial) will be imparted during residence at the home, in subordination to the primary object of the Home, viz., the health of the weak and sickly. Any soldier's child, with the following exceptions, can be admitted; those ineligible are:-

Children of mixed parentage.

Children suffering from contagious disorders.

Children under three years, unless accompanied by an elder sister.

Boys over 12 year of age.

A limited number of girls over 15 years of age will be admitted free, with the object of training them for service as nurse-maids in ladies' families; they will assist in looking after the younger children.

The scale of fees payable, including Government allowance, of Rs 2-8 per child, is follows:-

Staff Sergeant's 1st child, Rs.6; 2nd, Rs.5; 3rd, Rs.5-0

Sergeant's	"	" 5	" 4	"	" 4-0
Corporal's	"	" 4	" 3	"	" 3-0
Private's	"	" 3	" 3	"	" 2-8

Applications for admission of children must be accompanied by a Medical Certificate, and a roll giving the following information, which must be sent through the Commanding Officer:-

Name and age of each child.

Rank of father.

Religion of parents.

Whether of thorough European parentage.

Any peculiar weakness of constitution.

Applications for admission to be sent to the Superintendent, from whom particulars regarding clothes, bedding, & c., can be ascertained – not later than the 10th April.

Government has sanctioned the travelling at the public expense of these children with the necessary guardians to and from the Home, under Government Letter in Military Department, No. 99, of 4th May 1877; also G. O. No. 82 of 1878, and Pay Code, para. 2030a.

Passage warrants to Saharunpur only are necessary. Arrangements for carriage hence to Masuri being made by the Superintendent. According to the Report for 1883, issued immediately before this book goes to Press, the institution still flourishes.

∞∞∞

SIND-PANJAB AND DELHI RAILWAY COMPANY'S HILL SCHOOL. – This School has somewhat similar aims to those of the Summer Home for Soldiers' Children, and is, practically, a charitable institution. The last report states that the institution began in 1877 with 27 children, and that it now accommodates upwards of 40; while if certain proposed extensions were carried out, it is calculated that the numbers would increase to 100. Dr. McConaghey, the former Civil Surgeon of Masuri, reports that the situation of the School is all that could be desired for children who have resided for a number of years in the plains. "The altitude, which is about 5 ½ thousand feet, is below the ordinary snow range in the winter months, so that the children might remain at Fair Lawn, with decided benefit to their health throughout the year." The school at present provides no separation for boys and girls, which is most necessary, and it is contemplated to erect another building for boys. The Committee are: Mr. R. Bocquet, C.I.E., President; Colonel Medley, R.E.; Mr. J. Lightfoot; Mr. E. Benedict; Mr. David Ross, C.I.E.; Mr. C. Sandiford; Dr. Center; with Mrs. David Ross, as Honorary Secretary. The object of the institution is to give an elementary English education to the children of the Sind-Panjab and Delhi Railway employés, at a reasonable cost, with the advantages of a hill climate. The terms to parents compare disadvantageously with those of the "Summer Home for Soldiers'

Children," and appear to be rather high. They are as follows:- Rs. 10 per mensem for each child whose parents draw pay under Rs. 100; Rs. 12 per mensem for each child whose parent's pay ranges between Rs. 100 and Rs. 150; Rs. 15 per mensem for each child whose parent receives Rs. 150 and over. A reduction is made for two or more of one family. The fees include all charges usually termed extras. The rules state that no children will be admitted under four years, and no boys above twelve years of age. The school fees are deducted monthly from the Pay Bills by the Audit Office. A month's notice of removal is required, or payment of a month's fees, except in case of sickness. Holidays are allowed during the months of December and January, but arrangements are made that children who do not avail themselves of the holidays can remain at the School. Mr. J. Buchart is the superintendent or teacher, and he is assisted by Mrs. Buchart and Miss Clarke, and the institution has gone on smoothly under their management.

༄༅།།

HOTELS. – Although Hotels may, in a certain sense, come under the broad denomination of "institutions," they are, for obvious reasons, scarcely subject of comment, good, bad, or indifferent, although neither of the two latter adjectives are, the writer believes, applicable to any of the hotels of Masuri. Even if comparisons could be drawn, with strict deference to the rules of literary propriety, the writer's ignorance and inexperience would disqualify him from offering criticism of any kind. Even if it were not so, to extol or disparage, in the case of, in a sense, rival institutions, would be quite out of good taste in a book of this sort. They are 'Himalaya' Hotel, which Mr. Andrew Wilson, author of the "Abode of Snow," remarked was "the best hotel he had met with in India.' There is also that old-established hostelry, the 'Masuri Hotel,' which enjoys the favor of a large following; the 'Charleville' Hotel, which, under recent management, has become popular; and the 'Woodville' Hotel, where satisfactory accommodation may be found.

༄༅།།

SCHOOLS. – Their name is legion, but as in this case, too, comparisons would be odious, the details of each must be left to its own announcements. It may be remarked, however, that Masuri is fast becoming one vast seminary, and may be termed the Edinburgh of India.

༄༅།།

LANDAUR.

Landaur commences at the Police Chauki, at the Grand Parade, as it is most inappropriately called, and near the General Post Office. Here also commences that important business mart, the Landaur Bazaar. Here are the large native merchant's shops, the clothe merchants, and the native grain merchants, &c., &c., all under the control of the Cantonment Magistrate, the Colonel Commandant for the time being. A nerik, or price current, for all kinds of commodities is published weekly. This bazaar is frequently crowded by Europeans in the evening, and a good deal of business is done.

There are upward of 240 houses and shops in the Sadar Bazaar, Landaur, besides other business shops scattered throughout the station. The average native population in the season is 2,500. The Landaur Bazaar is one of the best supplied Bazaars in India. Many of the native merchants purchase their goods through agents in England, France, America, and other countries, so that goods of nearly all descriptions can always be obtained in Landaur.

At the eastern end of the Bazaar, the ascent of the Landaur Hill commences. At the beginning of the rise there is a cluster of European residences which are let at more moderate rents than those further up the hill. At an early point in the ascent, the road up to the Landaur Church branches off right and left. The left is the shorter way, but it is very steep; that to the right is the better road, with an easy ascent all the way up. When we arrive at the Church, it may be said we are in Landaur proper. The large open space under the Church is flanked by the Orderly-Room, the Cantonment Magistrate's Katcheri, and the Library. To the left, over a wooden bridge, is the commencement of the Landaur Mall, a very pleasant walk or ride, passing between the Protestant and Roman Catholic Cemeteries, and coming out by the Guard-Room. A sharp turn to the right will bring the visitors to what used to be called the Raquet Court, but now the Landaur Theatre, where amateur theatricals and other entertainments are given. Further on up the same hill is the Sergeant's Mess, and still further on the open piece of ground above the Roman Catholic Chapel, from which, as has already been mentioned, a fine view of the snows may be obtained. This is one of the two highest points in Landaur. Returning to Guard-Room, and proceeding to the left, the road to Lal Tiba is reached. Lal Tiba is the other highest point in Landaur. The maps do not give the altitude of the two particular points mentioned, but it cannot be less than 7,400 feet above sea level! Lal Tiba possesses the advantage of offering a splendid view of the Dun. From these points, and, indeed, from any point of Landaur proper, the visitor looks down upon Masuri proper. Even the highest knoll of the Camel's back must be about 470 feet below Lal Tiba. Continuing on the same road under Lal Tiba, we reach the Landaur

Hospital, for the medical treatment of the soldiers, of course.

The number of private houses in Landaur is 80, inclusive of Woodstock School and the Imperial (now "Oriental") Hotel. In addition to the above, there are 25 Government Bungalows, used as soldiers' barracks. Eight private houses are also rented for the accommodation of the soldiers.

The numbers of the different ranks of the military which find accommodation in these various quarters are as follows: - From 11th April to 15th November, annually; officers 7, men 226, women 23, children about 50 - total 306. From 16th November to 10th April annually; officers 2, men 70, women 6, and about 15 children – total 93.

The Commandant, the Station Staff Officer, and the Chaplain hold their respective offices for two years only, and, at the expiration of that time, in each individual case, fresh officers are appointed. The remainder of the staff, – i.e., the Medical officer, the Staff Sergeant-Major, the Quarter-Master Sergeant, and the Orderly-Room Sergeant, are practically permanent appointments. Changes, however, are not infrequent with regard to the medical officer.

The present Commandant of the Depôt is Lieut.-Col. J. P. Campbell, who should have vacated his appointment in March. He has been especially popular with all classes, and is succeeded by Colonel C. de N. O. Stockwell. The Station Staff Officer is Captain Richardson (40th) and the Revd. P. Nicolas, the Chaplain, who should have given up charge in December 1883. The other Staff Officers are:-Surgeon-Major Wilkes, Sergeant-Major W. J. Herbison, Quarter-Master Sergeant G. Stevenson, and Orderly-Room Sergeant J. F. de L. Evans.

The criminal jurisdiction of the Commanding Officer extends to the trial of persons for breaches of cantonment rules under Cantonments Act III of 1880.

A Chaukidari Tax is levied under the Chaukidari Act XX of 1856. A House Tax is leviable up to 5 per cent on actual rentals, half being payable by the landlord, and half by the tenant. For 1883, 4 per cent only has been levied.

As to sanitary arrangements, the Cantonment Committee arrange for the removal of all refuse & c., daily from private houses, to the filth pits. No charge, other than those mentioned above, is made on this account against the landlords or tenants. The Cantonment is at all times in a very clean and sanitary condition, no less than three soldiers being employed during the season in a daily inspection of the Bazaars and private compounds, in order to see if they are kept clean, and that no refuse or filth is strewn about. Landaur is a popular sanitarium and from its altitude is healthy and most pleasant place to reside in.

MUSSOORIE MEMOIRS:

A PICTURE DIARY

Charcoal-sellers like this one were a
common sight up until the 1960s.
They went extinct with the advent
of the New Forest Conservation Act.

On Camel's Back road stands
the Skating Rink—
a rendezvous for lovers.

Gulam Mohammed merchant's advertisement in 1884 read: 'Begs to inform Residents and
Visitors to Mussoorie and Landour that he receives direct from England Weekly stores
 of every description, thereby enabling him to guarantee every thing being perfectly fresh
and of the first quality'.

(FACING PAGE): The sharp incline of the Mall Road near Kulri Bazaar opposite the
Methodist Church still draws the visitor's attention to a row of eateries.

Methodist Church on the slope of the Mall Road has been restored to its normal glory.

Kellogg Church doubles as the Landour Language school attracting students from around the world who come to learn Hindi, Urdu and Punjabi.

A fine aspect of the Mall lined with acetylene gas lamps
shows the Mall Road as it was meant to be—
just a promenade for visitors and residents alike.

View of Mall from Kalisa Cottage. Of those early days old timers moan:
'Ah! It was so clean, you could almost eat an omelette off the road!'

*Travellyan & Clarke Exchange Building on the Mall,
in the days of its glory at the turn of the 19th century.*

This fashionable shopping mall was built in the 1920s. Earlier, on its grounds was the winter bungalow of Raja Pahari Wilson in Dehradun.

Lt Gen Sir John Bennet Hearsey in the regalia of the
2nd Bengal Irregular Cavalry (circa 1817) who bought the 'pergana'
of the Doon on June 22nd 1811 from Raja Sudarshan Shah of Tehri
for Rs 3005/-, a sale not accepted by the British.

(FACING PAGE, TOP): On the grounds of today's St Joseph's Academy in Dehradun, Captain
Young built his home and his wife's horse is seen in this early sketch.

(FACING PAGE, BELOW): The first train steamed into the Dun in 1899, run by the
Oudh and Rohilkhand Railway on a line that skirted the east end of the Siwaliks.

Halfway House, Jharipani, was on the old bridle path to Mussoorie, literally halfway between the valley and the hill station.

The old township of Rajpur was once the overnight watering hole in the valley of the Dun.

A view from the gorge near Wild Flower Hall with the Maharaja of Kapurthala's magnificent Chateau in the background.

(*FACING PAGE*): *Kempty Falls: The pristine beauty of the Kempty Falls, in the 1920s, along the road to Yamuna Bridge enroute to the Yamunotri shrine, is a marked contrast to the kitsch architechture of today.*

The old Happy Valley Club was at the end of the flat below the Charleville Hotel, whose turrets are seen on the right of frame. It was advertised as: 'The hotel is known to be situated in the healthiest part of Mussoorie... It is the only Hotel that can boast of having extensive grounds well-wooded with pleasant walks around, while the views of the snows and surrounding hills cannot be equalled.'